BOSS SOUNDS
CLASSIC SKINHEAD REGGAE

By Marc Griffiths

S.T. PUBLISHING

To my wife, Delia, who is certainly not a fan of skinhead reggae, and my four year old son, Luke, who certainly will be if I have anything to do with it.

Boss Sounds - Classic Skinhead Reggae (pbk)

© Marc Griffiths, 1995

ISBN 1 898927 20 0

Published by S.T. Publishing, Scotland.

Printed by Pyramid Press, England.

A CIP catalogue record for this book is available from the British Library.

S.T. PUBLISHING
P.O. Box 12, Dunoon, Argyll. PA23 7BQ. Scotland.
Purveyors Of Street Literature For A Good Few Years Now

BOSS SOUNDS
CLASSIC SKINHEAD REGGAE

INTRODUCTION - Author's Foreword

Readers of *Skinhead Times* were given the chance to by advance copies of *Boss Sounds*. The first 60 people to do so were David Lopez, Vincent Bichard, Nick Brady, Dite Burns, Nick Hewitson, Graham Hook, P.R. Elvy, Alan Calver, P. Cummings, Phil Minton, Paul Oakman, Arnaud Nee, G.J. Kelt, Vincent Lyte, Frank Van Rijsingen, Einar Vadstein, Tom Marcowka, Christine Owen, Heinrich Ariss, Serge Schryvers, Katia and Toks, Alex Gramlich, Aaron Hendrix, Wayne Dymond, Patrice Boisseau, Bianchi Folco, Alfonso Sacristan, P.A. Rees, José Morte Aragones, Paul Jameson, Oliver Söhn, Karen Jung, André Remmert, Kurt Wetzel, Wayne Frankland, Pete Roper, Jan Willem Koolen, Manfred Pollak, Dominick Bruno Jr, Jens Svane, Franck Etchegaray, Philippe Jonart, Jordi Ramirez, Steve Harrington, Melissa Mackie, Neil Cameron, P. Nichol, Peter Levo, Frédéric Fombaron, Kari Lehto, Arne Mathingsdal, Harald Steen, Pieter Neefs, Charly McBride, Lee Murphy, Ulf Stammwitz, Sander de Wilde, Emmanuel Boulay, Stefan Jost and Jacquel Runnalls.

CRAMON'S ENTERPRISES

with

PINEAPPLE RECORDS

proudly presents

DESMOND DEKKER

in a grand

REGGAE
SOUL CONCERT

and

DANCE

at

ACTON HALL

Acton, Friday, December 12th, 1969

plus

LAUREL AITKEN
AND THE
NIYHA SHUFFLE

Tickets 1 gn. Licensed bar available. For advance tickets apply to Cramon's Enterprises, 40 Church Street, N.W.8. Telephone 262 7800

Thanks to the following for their help with this book - Barry Plummer, Nick Welsh, Ossi Münnig, Simon Buckland, Laurence Cane-Honeysett, Mike Atherton, Herve Etchegaray, Mark Brennan, Kev Avery, Roger Nolda and Dave Drew.

As Marc Griffiths states in his foreword, we would welcome any additions or corrections to this book for use in future editions. You can send them to S.T. Publishing, P.O. Box 12, Dunoon, Argyll. PA23 7BQ. Scotland.

AUTHOR'S FOREWORD

When **George Marshall asked me whether I had ever thought about writing a book on reggae, the answer was that it had certainly crossed my mind on more than one occasion.** Even during the period when reggae was at its peak, there were only a few reference items published on the origins of the music and the people who made up what *Blues And Soul* magazine termed "The Reggae Scene".

The first thing I remember reading which attempted to put the music of Jamaica into perspective was a slim booklet entitled, *Reggae, A People's Music* by Rolston Kallyndyr and Henderson Dalrymple, published back in '73. This contained vast quantities of obvious contradictions, errors and inaccuracies which seem to have been passed down through the years and accepted as gospel. Otherwise, there was an article in an edition of *Rock File* on rude reggae written by Carl Gayle; something in one of the Sunday magazines on sound systems; and the odd interview with a reggae artist in *Blues And Soul* or *Black Music*. But nothing substantial has ever been written about the peak rock steady and reggae periods between 1967 and 1973 and, in particular, the appeal of the music to one of its largest customers - the skinheads.

At the back of my mind has always been a desire to try and pull the loose ends of the '67-'73 reggae world together into one large book which would be of value to devotees like myself. I knew this wouldn't be an easy task because, for a start, there aren't many original skinheads still around who can tell us what being a reggae fan in '69 was like, so in the final analysis it still comes down largely to relying on often suspect second hand knowledge. On the other hand, Roger Dalke's excellent series of *Ska To Reggae* discographies has certainly improved the information available on many early records in terms of labels, producers and artists.

Like many people, I first became interested in reggae through hearing *Israelites*. I knew it had a different sound to other stuff in the charts and that the local skinheads went mad over it, but at only eight and a bit years old I hadn't appreciated that this was actually "reggae". During the summer of 1970, a Burmese kid joined my school class and we often exchanged views on the latest reggae and soul sounds. He had three older brothers who were into reggae, and one ran a sound system and built speaker boxes for other sound system operators.

It wasn't long before I was invited round to his place to listen to records on strange labels like Gas, High Note and Bamboo by people I'd never heard of before like Laurel Aitken, Derrick Morgan and Monty Morris. Hearing these gave me a useful lead into the best discs to pick up when one of the main reggae distributors went into liquidation and sold the bulk of their stock to Tesco stores. At just ten new pence a throw (!), I was able to pick up classics like *If It Don't Work Out* by Pat Kelly on Gas, *Cool Down* by Winston Hinds on Camel, *We Were Lovers* by Patsy on High Note, *Magic Touch* by Junior Soul (Murvin) on Big Shot; and many other gems.

The Slipped Disc in Clapham Junction (which was a few doors away from where Dub Vendor is now) was also selling off unsold Melodisc stock at 10p a shot. Prince Buster's *Johnny Cool* on the gold Fab label was one of many worthwhile purchases I made from this shop and most of these 10p records are still with me to this day. They were also very good investments for a young kid with only 50p a week pocket money - new singles at the time sold for around 45p each.

Apart from buying these early classics, I also collected Trojan LPs in the TBL and TTL series (generally *Tighten Up* and *Club Reggae* volumes). At 99p each they were about 50p cheaper than full-price albums on major labels. So for a youngster on a limited budget, buying reggae was definitely more economical than having to save up for weeks for the latest T Rex LP! But by 1972, there were plenty of places to pick up late Sixties unplayed reggae and rock steady for what, even then, was peanuts. I once shelled out 75p for a copy of the original *Greatest Jamaican Beat* album on UK Treasure Isle at one of the many emporiums dotted around London. Who could have foreseen that an item like this would fetch prices in the region of £75 some twenty years later?

Growing up in a West Indian community like Balham in South West London also had its advantages. Apart from being a skinhead stronghold, it also boasted two excellent reggae specialist shops, namely Musik City (in the underground station) and Record Corner in nearby Bedford Hill. The latter was where I bought a copy of Eric Donaldson's *Cherry O Baby*, which was the first "current" reggae 45 I acquired. Just a few miles north east of Balham was Brixton, which boasted at least five reggae shops within a minute's walk from each other, including Desmond's Hip City, Musik City, Joe's (Mansano) Shack and Music Box. The boss sounds of reggae echoed from shop to shop through Granville Arcade and the market.

Sadly, most of the Musik City shops began to close around the end of '73. Record Corner had started to specialise in soul instead of reggae by about '76 and so the number of outlets for the music (certainly in South West London anyway) had declined from its peak period in the late Sixties and early Seventies.

I had become vaguely interested in dub and roots music by '75 but, even then, the early sounds never lost their appeal for me. If you were a white guy looking to meet white girls, the sound system dances which played all-night dub did not provide a particularly good mating ground. This was very much a black man's music and, frankly, it bored me stupid after listening to it for more than a few hours.

I then became disenchanted with late Seventies reggae until Two Tone came along, by which time I'd become a fully-fledged skinhead. After Two Tone had fizzled out, Oi! became the favoured skinhead music. Now, Oi! certainly wasn't my bag (not that I've anything against it) and after the Southall fiasco it had, for obvious (but very wrong reasons) become particularly dangerous to walk London's streets dressed in skinhead style. But although I've ceased to be a skinhead, I've never lost my enthusiasm for the great sounds of rock steady and early reggae.

Like most types of modern music, prices of original copies of these records have really shot up in the last several years. Singles can still be found for reasonable amounts - there aren't in fact too many that go for more than £15 a throw and compared with prices for original rock 'n' roll, northern soul and psychedelia, "our" music comes out very favourably. Increased demand, particularly from overseas collectors, has made inflated prices inevitable.

Also, as so much of the original vinyl is now (characteristically) in poor condition, many dealers attempt to put a premium on discs in good nick. But a knackered Studio One single, with no centre and a scrawl all over the label, might still be priced up at a few quid even though it's worth 50p in anyone's collection. Most dealers know the position. If you pass up that shitty copy now, you might never see another one. On the other hand, a lot of them know next to nothing about the music and buy completely on the basis of label. I knew one dealer who paid a few hundred quid for a large quantity of 45s on labels like Hala-gala, Blue Beat, Dice, and Island. Unfortunately for him, it was a prime collection of the duffest cuts on the labels and he couldn't shift them for love nor money.

Album-wise however, prices have spiralled out of all proportion. In general, copies

BLUEBEAT'S GREATEST FANS—THE SKINHEADS

DESPITE the fact that the very likeable Mr. Stephen Ellis of the Love Affair lays claim to being the original skinhead, they're not in general a lovable lot!

Skinheads are the new wave mods - and like many of their predecessors, bluebeat is THEIR music.

A skinhead is easy to recognise. Making a grand stand against hippies, long-hairs, drop-outs and all similar breed, the skinhead sports a haircut even shorter than the mod. In fact it's a good down to earth crew-cut.

Fashionwise, as they say, the skinhead also sticks out from the crowd. Boots (sort of Army style things without the metal) stamp non-chalantly across the tufted carpet, and jeans three sizes too small with no need for moral or

material support are held up by good old fashioned braces of all styles and hues! Black eyes and other minor scars are predominant, for the skinheads are not by nature a peaceable pack.

This aside, the skinheads of Britain are considered the experts on blue beat 1969. Some of them know far more about the music than their West Indian colleagues.

Skinheads by nature are uniform. They all look alike, they all move around in bands, and they all follow each other. So it could be said they like the uniformity of bluebeat.

of original early LPs (the more popular Trojan titles excepted) have always been relatively few and far between. Back in the Sixties and Seventies, a visit to the local reggae store was a full afternoon out for a West Indian with a few quid in his pocket. Endless latest sounds would be spun and the punters would amass a small pile of 45s (or even just one!) for purchase, depending obviously on which ones they liked. Although the cost comparison must come into the equation somewhere, buying a reggae album never unfortunately offered this sort of hours-long buying experience. LPs generally served the needs of a much smaller group of customers, and compilation LPs usually contained material which would've been old hat to a hip young black guy.

One point I would like to make concerns the references to prices in this book. I'm not trying to talk up prices when I say that a certain disc can fetch a vast amount. I'm in the business of buying them myself and I do know what they can go for. It's a fact of life that German and Japanese collectors can generally pay five times more than anyone else can afford for a certain sought after item. Whatever happens in the future, I hope the bastards flog all their records back here when they no longer want them!

Anyway, that's part of my life story together with some background on my experience of collecting. In this book, you'll find in-depth coverage of the many labels that issued the music, the people behind the mixing desks, different styles and trends, and a personal overview of all the boss sounds from a long-time reggae devotee.

What isn't here - and I freely admit it - is a great deal of information about the artists themselves. A new book, *Who's Who Of Reggae* (Guiness) covers a lot of this ground anyway, as do many articles in other books and fanzines issued in the recent past. My book focuses more on the vinyl side of things and is almost completely unique in doing so. If you've read (and you should have) George Marshall's *Spirit of '69* book, you'll have noted his skinhead reggae feature. What I've actually done is to expand this feature one hundred fold. Skinheads and fans of early reggae needed a comprehensive book, and I hope it serves the purpose well. I've done my level best to get all my facts and figures right but letters drawing my attention to any inaccuracies and omissions would be perfectly welcome. Honest!

Much respect is due to George Marshall for both inspiring and encouraging me to take on what is generally considered to be a minefield as a serious project. I'd also like to say a word of thanks to two decent and reputable dealers, namely Dave Russell and his Muzik City reggae stall, and Steve McGlashan, both of whom have kept me well supplied with good reggae vinyl for many years. Thanks also goes to Fred Dornier for his consistent flow of correspondence (when is that bloody fanzine going to be ready?!). To wrap up the "thanks and praise" bit, I'd also like to pass on my support and best wishes to all non-racist skinheads everywhere.

Marc Griffiths
London, May 1995.

CHAPTER ONE
REGGAE HISTORY
From The Beginning

To understand how the reggae beat came about, it is necessary to go back to the earliest roots of Jamaican music (although I'll keep it as brief as possible, as I'm sure this won't be everybody's cup of tea). Before the mid-Fifties, mento and calypso were the island's most popular music forms, along with country and western. Mento was a traditional home-grown sound played acoustically, while calypso originated in Trinidad. As for country and western, many Jamaicans have always had an ear for the "heart warming" sounds of the likes of Jim Reeves and Hank Williams. There were also numerous orchestras in Jamaica playing swing, jazz and jive music.

When Tom "The Great" Sebastian started the island's first sound system around 1950, the discs played were dance music in the form of American rhythm and blues. The hottest artists were Louis Jordan, Jackie Brenston (check out his *Rocket 88*), Wynonie Harris, Johnny Ace and, last but by no means least, Fats Domino. Neither mento or calypso (which by then was massively popular in the US courtesy of Harry Belafonte) were particularly good for dancing to, and the sound system patrons wanted the faster pace of the early R & B "race" sounds, which were by then being imported to the island from the States and could be picked up over the airwaves courtesy of the US radio station, WINZ. Other sound system operators in business by 1957 were Duke Reid, Duke Vin, Sir Coxsone and Nicks.

By 1957 however, authentic black R & B had become pretty much a dying art. Most black artists were by then making records which were, to some degree, crossing over to the white market. The likes of Big Joe Turner, Fats Domino, Nappy Brown and Clyde McPhatter were still turning out good records but, to all intents and purposes, they were rock 'n' roll, and a fair amount of them were now getting into the US Billboard Hot 100. With the source of authentic American R & B records drying up, the main sound system operators (generally Coxsone and Duke Reid) started producing their own records using local artists like Laurel Aitken, Owen Gray and Theo Beckford initially for exclusive use on their own systems as "specials".

Over the years, there has been some speculation as to when the earliest JA produced discs were released. For example, the story goes that Owen Gray's *On the Beach* (Coxsone) was first put out in Jamaica in 1956, and that Laurel Aitken's *Judgement Day* (Duke Reid) and Theo Beckford's *Easy Snappin'* (Coxsone) were both issued around 1957. If this is so, the first discs of West Indian origin to be released in the UK would by then have been a few years old. Clearly, there was obviously sufficient demand for these "early" sounds from the West Indian immigrant population in the UK.

The music itself was prototype ska, and had a loping back beat derived from R&B, boogie and the blues. In fact, were it not for the primitive nature of the productions, many could almost have passed themselves off as US originals.

There was little or no mixing down and the instruments were fed directly into the recording "as miked". This often meant that tenor saxes, horns and trombones would boom out unexpectedly at much too high a level (Ruddy And Sketto's *Mr Postman* is an excellent example of this).

For anyone wishing to acquaint themselves with these early sounds, I've compiled the following list of 10 UK issued 45s which in my view are all good examples of the genre:

1. *Bouncing Woman* - **Laurel Aitken** (Blue Beat BB 52)
2. *Walking Down King Street* - **Theo Beckford** (Blue Beat BB 87)
3. *Little Sheila / Boogie In My Bones* - **Laurel Aitken** (Starlite ST 011)*
4. *Bartender* - **Laurel Aitken** (Blue Beat BB 40)
5. *Easy Snapping* - **Theo Beckford** (Blue Beat BP 15)
6. *Fat Man* - **Derrick Morgan** (Blue Beat BB 7)
7. *Mr Postman* - **Ruddy And Sketto** (Dice CC 10)
8. *You Got Me Rockin'* - **Laurel Aitken & Hyacinth** (Dice CC 1)
9. *More Whiskey* - **Laurel Aitken** (Blue Beat BB 25)
10. *Morning Train* - **Errol Dixon** (Island WI 017)
* Later re-issued on Island WI 198.

Probably the first independent label to issue West Indian music in the UK was Melodisc (I stress independent because there were several calypso 78s issued on London, a subsidiary of Decca, around 1954). Melodisc was a long-established label which had begun issuing black music in the form of calypso around 1957, and its forays into the world of jazz and blues were even earlier. It issued calypso 45s by Lord Kitchener (and a 10" LP) and Lord Melody from around 1958. Melodisc's Blue Beat subsidiary was set up at the tail end of 1960 to deal specifically with JA music (with a few exceptions). Starlite, a subsidiary of the long-established jazz-oriented label, Esquire, also begun issuing Jamaican music between 1960-61.

At this stage, small independent labels in the UK

numbered only a handful. Melodisc and Esquire were among the largest of them, but most of the major UK labels did go some way to cater for West Indian tastes with the issue of calypso material by the likes of George Browne (EMI / Parlophone), Mighty Terror (EMI / Capitol) and Frank Holder (Pye Nixa). Melodisc in fact created the Kalypso label around 1960 to deal specifically with calypso and mento sounds.

The run of JA sounds on Starlite was fairly short-lived and included artists such as Laurel Aitken, Wilfred (Jackie) Edwards, Higgs And Wilson, The Jiving Juniors (with Derrick Harriott in the line-up) and Keith And Enid. Blue Beat, which was run by Emille Shalitt, then practically dominated the blue beat (as ska was then known in the UK) market until mid-1962.

Apart from Blue Beat and Starlite, the major source of JA music at this time was to be found on imported discs, and as many as 15-20,000 a month were reputedly shipped into the UK. Many of the early retail outlets for the music here were in fact shops specialising in afro-cosmetics, wigs, and shipping services from Jamaica - the sale of records was merely a sideline in what were all-in-one stores offering a multitude of services to West Indian immigrants. Dyke And Dryden in East London's Dalston market was one such shop, and 30 years on is now one of the UK's major retailers of afro-cosmetic products!

A number of smaller labels had started up by the end of 1962 and these are mentioned in chapter two. Island Records was the next major label to start issuing West Indian music in the UK. It was run by white Jamaican Chris Blackwell from 108 Cambridge Road in London's Kilburn Park (now long since demolished) which apparently housed a record shop run by Lee Gopthal (more about him later) and a recording studio. Having been born and raised in Jamaica, Blackwell was in a good position to issue West Indian recordings in the UK.

Blue beat, or ska, changed relatively little until rock steady became the hottest sound in JA around 1966. As this book is not intended to cover ska in any depth, the interested reader can whet his or her appetite with the following ten discs (assuming they can get them!):

1. *Guns of Navarone / Marcus Garvey* - **The Skatalites / Bongo Man** (Island WI 168) 1965
2. *Madness* - **Prince Buster** (Blue Beat BB 170) 1963
3. *Carry Go, Bring Come* - **Justin Hinds & The Dominoes** (Island WI 154) 1964
4. *It's Burke's Law* - **Prince Buster** (Blue Beat BB 309) 1965
5. *Blazing Fire* - **Derrick Morgan** (Island WI 051) 1963
6. *One Eyed Giant* - **Baba Brooks** (Ska Beat JB 220) 1965*
7. *Broadway Jungle* - **The Flames** (Island WI 139) 1964
8. *Thirty Pieces Of Silver* - **Prince Buster** (Blue Beat BB 248) 1964
9. *National Dance* - **Derrick & Patsy Morgan** (Island WI 224) 1965
10. *Watermelon Man* - **Baba Brooks** (R & B / Ska Beat JB 125) 1963
* Later reissued on Ska Beat JB 268 .

Sometime during the first half of 1966, the tempo of the ska rhythm began to slow down into a beat which came to be known as "rock steady". This was possibly in response to dancers' requests for a slower music during that year's heatwave in JA, but may also have been because ska had reached its full potential after five or so years of being the number one sound, and something new was being demanded.

Ska still retained its popularity in the UK throughout part of '67 (witness the highly successful *Club Ska '67* volumes that year, and Prince Buster's *Al Capone* on Blue Beat and The Skatalites' *Guns of Navarone* on Island, both of which were

Above: Born Cecil Campbell, Prince Buster was the king of ska.

already two years old). Rock steady records were in any case not being released here until several months after they had appeared in JA. For example, Ken Boothe's *Home, Home, Home* on Coxsone was issued in Jamaica during December 1966, but didn't see release on these shores until around the middle of '67. The new music did however make it into the U.K. national charts that year in the form of Desmond Dekker's *007* on Pyramid and The Ethiopians' *Train To Skaville* on Rio. Initially, both these discs were massive hits in the clubs and discos, and it was largely through these two mediums that they took off nationally.

By this time, Island and Doctor Bird were the major UK labels in the market, with Rio (which was also part of the Doctor Bird Group) and R&B's Ska Beat label following a little way behind. Blue Beat had largely lost its grip on the market and was releasing fewer discs than previously. However, 1967 and the dawning of the rock steady era heralded two new companies which would later supplant all four labels: Trojan (initially an Island subsidiary) and Pama.

The background to Beat & Commercial Co. (Lee Gopthal's distribution company) and Island / Trojan is actually a pretty complicated affair. The operation was in fact a partnership between Chris Blackwell of Island, who pressed B & C's discs, and Lee Gopthal, who handled the distribution and retail side. Gopthal, an accountant by training, had been involved with Jamaican music since 1964 and was a long-time associate of Blackwell. Gopthal had by 1967 built up quite a sizeable chain of specialist shops selling JA music to London's West Indian communities, namely Musicland and Musik City (although Musicland may in fact have been more pop-oriented since it had shops outside London's ethnic areas). The first subsidiary labels created by Island to deal exclusively with rock steady were Coxsone and Studio One (for C.S. Dodd productions), and Treasure Isle (for Duke Reid productions) in the early months of 1967.

Trojan was the subsidiary label which Island created following Studio One, Coxsone and Treasure Isle. The first Trojan 45 (*Judge Sympathy* by Duke Reid & The Freedom Singers) was issued in July 1967, and the following ten releases were all produced by Duke Reid. The Amalgamated and Blue Cat labels were added to the Island / B & C roster around April 1968, with High Note, Down Town, Duke and Big Shot coming into being several months later. Gopthal broke B & C away from Island around mid-1968 when Trojan's second series - the TR 600s - was started and Trojan then became an independent company (although Island still maintained some sort of business interest for several years). Trojan / B & C (as it was soon to be known) took all the Island subsidiaries (such as Studio One, Coxsone etc.) with it. With Gopthal as chairman of the new company, he now had complete control over what to release and, given his retail empire, where it was to be sold.

The Amalgamated label dealt almost exclusively with Joe Gibbs productions. High Note dealt mainly with productions from Sonia Pottinger, but both Blue Cat and Big Shot released discs from a variety of producers covering late rock steady and early reggae sounds. Down Town dealt 100% with productions by UK artist and producer Dandy (aka Robert Thompson), and Duke began (as might be

expected) with some Duke Reid productions. There were no hard and fast rules however - some of these subsidiary labels started with a particular producer's material and then chopped and changed later on. The reason for this is completely unclear. Also, certain Doctor Bird, Pyramid and Rio tracks appeared on Island compilations, which was strange in that the Doctor Bird Group was reputedly an independent concern run by a guy called Graeme Goodall. Island / B & C was certainly the distributor of Doctor Bird Group product (I did say that this was a complicated business!), but this suggests perhaps that there was some other tenuous link between the companies, or perhaps the tracks were simply licensed by Island.

Chapter three looks at the Trojan / B & C subsidiaries and their releases in more detail, but so successful were many records on these labels that Jackpot (mainly for Bunny Lee productions), Clandisc (for Clancy Eccles productions), Explosion (initially mainly for Derrick Harriott productions), Song Bird (which later on became Trojan's outlet for Derrick Harriott material), Grape (for UK productions), Gayfeet (to supplement Sonia Pottinger's High Note outlet), and Upsetter (for 100% Lee Perry productions), were all added to Trojan's expanding empire at various times during 1969.

Above: The Pioneers outside Music House, once home of Trojan Records

Album-wise, Trojan really caught Joe Public's attention with its first volume of the hugely successful *Tighten Up* series in the opening months of '69. The album contained Trojan's biggest selling singles of 1968 and, although the tracks were obviously rather out of date by the time of release, it sold by the cartload with its attractive price tag of 14/6 (about 75p now, and half the cost of a full-price album when released). The famous second volume was issued late in '69 and reached number two in the national album charts, at which point the powers that be decided that budget price LPs should be eliminated from the listings and hence it disappeared from the charts after just three weeks!

By late 1969, Trojan / B & C was the dominant company in the reggae marketplace and was getting UK chart action with some of its 45 and LP releases (eg Jimmy Cliff, The Pioneers, Harry J All Stars, The Upsetters, Tony Tribe, and the *Tighten Up Volume 2* and *This Is Desmond Dekker* albums). In fact, at one time, Trojan owned or distributed as many as 30 different labels through B & C. Trojan were also releasing more albums than any other reggae company, and its compilations tended to highlight the work of individual producers, whereas Pama's tended to be made up of "best sellers" or popular sides from the various subsidiary labels (such as *Gas' Greatest Hits* and *The Best of Camel*).

A little later on, Trojan was also in the business of resurrecting other companies' labels which, for whatever reason, had become defunct. The label had adopted several of the Doctor Bird group's subsidiaries such as Attack (from '70 until '78), Pyramid (between '73 and '74), as well as Island's old ska outlet, Black Swan ('70-'71). In fact, B & C's job as distributor had become the linchpin of the UK reggae industry.

As with Pama, things seemed to start going wrong for Trojan in the early Seventies. Most of its labels which issued material originated by UK production men - notably Joe (for Joe Mansano), Hot Rod (for Lambert Briscoe), Q (for Count Suckle) and J-Dan (for Dandy) - had long been dropped, suggesting perhaps that the skinheads, who went for the UK stuff in a big way, were on the way out. Trojan also pulled the plug on Clandisc, Dynamic, Big and Moodisc in '72, and an almighty 14 were scrapped in '73. By 1974, Trojan had only around 13 subsidiary labels left under its control.

The reasons for Trojan / B & C's downfall aren't clear, but as time went on the company was issuing less and less "quality" material. By the summer of '73, only about 70% of releases were JA products, with the balace containing an element of very weak UK material from the likes of The Peaches (*Seven Little Girls Sitting In The Back Seat*), The Breadcrumbs (*Nice One Cyril*), and Steve Collins (*Ding-a-ling Ting-a-ling*).

Trojan, like Pama, had also resorted to re-issuing earlier titles which seems to indicate that it was having trouble filling up its release sheets. The *Club Reggae* and *Tighten Up* series were singing their respective swansongs and we were treated to LPs of long-discarded out-takes such as those to be found on Clancy Eccles' *Top Of The Ladder* LP on Big Shot. Of course, without good solid 45s under its belt, the company was finding it difficult to release compilation albums of any quality. Some of the big name producers of the time like Bunny Lee and Lee Perry had little or no product issued on Trojan labels after '73 and found other outlets for their music. Some however, like Derrick Harriott, remained loyal to Trojan for several more years.

WHERE TO BUY IT

MOST shops now stock a limited selection of ska/rock steady/reggae records, especially with the increased interest in the music.

But unless your local record shop proprietor is particularly friendly you may find yourself not being able to hear the records before you buy them—or more likely you will probably have to order them specially.

However, to get really steeped in the music, you'll have to visit or write to a bluebeat specialist. Try one from the list below.

Webster's, 5a Extension Market, Shepherd's Bush, London.

Desmond's Hip City, 55 Atlantic Road, Brixton, London.

Joe's, 93 Granville Arcade, London, S.W.9.

Readings, 11 Station Approach, Clapham Junction.

Dereks, 5 Turnpike Lane, London, N.8.

Beverleys, 11 Model Market, Lewisham.

Dyke and Dryden, 43 West Green Road, Tottenham.

Paul Marsh, 24 Alexandre Road, Moss Side, Manchester.

Don Christie, 116 Ladypool Road, Sparkbrook, Birmingham 12.

A. R. Burns Ltd., 225a Chapel Town Road, Leeds 7.

Brian Harris, 104 Grove Lane, Birmingham 21.

All these, plus Musicland branches at Deptford, Willesden Green, Edgware, Kingston-on-Thames, Hounslow, Watford and Portobello Road

The short-lived Trojan Appreciation Society had folded by early '74 and the company seemed to be undergoing a major cost-cutting exercise. The press releases and Top 50 listings dried up and the chain of Musik City stores was trimmed to the bone. B & C Music collapsed in 1975, resulting in Trojan's distribution network being decimated. This, coupled with the label's inability to release JA music of a consistently high quality and its emphasis on UK-produced commercial sounds, was probably the beginning of the end of Trojan's first phase.

The company did however have UK Top Ten hits with two Ken Boothe sides in 1974, including *Everything I Own*, which had a four week run at the number one spot, and a further smash with John Holt's *Help Me Make It Through The Night* later in the year. Good business was being done with Holt's *Volts* albums and Tito Simon's *Monday Morning Feeling* single on Horse. Things must have been pretty bad though because even Ken Boothe's near-million selling single couldn't stop the rot from setting in. Trojan was sold in 1975 for £32,000, and again in 1985 but has only in the last six years regained its foothold in the market following a series of highly impressive compilations of archive material. So far as I know, Lee Gopthal still works on the fringes of the reggae business today.

Pama was started in late 1967 by the two eldest Palmer Brothers, Harry and Jeff, initially from a small office in South Harrow and then later from the premises of a record shop at 78 Craven Park Road in North London's Harlesden. According to Clancy Eccles, who had a number of his rock steady outings issued by the company early on, the brothers were primarily connected with the property business, and probably began the label initially as a sideline to their main business interests. The main Pama label concentrated largely on soul 45s leased from US

record companies, but by mid-1968 demand for JA sounds was such that it resulted in the creation of a number of subsidiary labels dealing exclusively with rock steady and reggae. Nu-Beat was the first, and its initial release, *Train To Vietnam*, by The Rudies was put out in July '68.

The Unity, Crab and Gas labels were all up and running by December '68, and Bullet, Camel, Punch, Escort and Success appeared the following year. The Palmer Brothers must have had

some association with Bunny Lee (or vice versa) because there were JA issues of material on Pama (such as *Festival Time* by Pat Kelly) and Unity (such as *River To*

17

The Bank by Derrick Morgan). Apart from UK Unity, which tended to release mainly Bunny Lee produced material, Pama and most of its subsidiaries hosted a hotch-potch of different producers, whereas many of Trojan / B & C's tended to showcase the talents of individual producers. Pama's two main exceptions were Escort (which dealt initially with Harry J productions) and Success (for 100% Rupie Edwards productions).

Pama, with its specially designed sleeves heralding "Boss Sounds From Pama - Party Music Specialists" had become Trojan's most serious rival by mid-'69. Max Romeo's *Wet Dream* had got into the national Top Ten without a single airplay, selling around 250,000 copies in the process. It followed hot on the heels of Desmond Dekker's *Israelites* on Doctor Bird's subsidiary label, Pyramid, thereby getting there before any of Trojan's discs. But by the end of '69, Trojan had garnered several national hits and Pama were losing the race in terms of nation-wide sales. So what went wrong for Pama?

The most likely answer is that Pama never had Lee Gopthal's ear for the sort of tune that would sell on a national scale. Skinheads were buying reggae in massive quantities - both on Pama and Trojan labels - but Trojan's hit singles, often with orchestral backing arrangements, were also selling to pop music fans. Pama's discs tended to retain their "ethnic" feel until late in 1970 when they too succumbed to the "reggae with strings" approach.

To illustrate this point, Pama's Escort label issued the original untampered with version of Bob and Marcia's *Young, Gifted And Black*. Trojan had also leased the song from Jamaican producer Harry J and got orchestra leader Johnny Arthey to add strings. The result? Pama's version completely bombed while Trojan's counterpart went Top Five. Even Pama's hasty attempt to introduce a rival UK-recorded version of the song by Denzil (Dennis) And Jennifer (Jones) was completely overshadowed by Trojan's effort.

Although Trojan was by far the most successful of the two companies on a national level, Pama issued hundreds of classic sides, many of which are now regarded as skinhead greats. Like Trojan, some of its singles (like Pat Kelly's seminal *How Long* on Gas) sold thousands of copies without getting a chart placing. Where Pama did surpass Trojan (although certainly not in terms of sales) was in the area of compilation LPs. The company designed its own sleeves and - unlike Trojan - wrote interesting back cover notes on some of its releases aimed very much at the potential UK buyer. The sleeve for volume one of the *This Is Reggae* set is a classic, showing as it does singer Dobby Dobson with assorted skinheads and rudies. Presumably though, all this effort had little effect on sales as by 1971 Pama merely aped Trojan by putting naked women on the covers and offering next to nothing in the way of sleeve notes!

Pama was still doing good business by 1972 but, like Trojan, seemed to be placing a great deal of emphasis on its UK productions. The material it was releasing by the likes of Denzil Dennis, The Freedom Singers, The Third Dimension and Fitzroy Sterling were selling next to nothing compared to earlier singles, and mountains of unsold copies were much later destined to end up for sale in Daddy Kool's London shop for a couple of quid a throw. The cover versions the company put out (such as Carl Levy's *Knock Three Times*, or Fitzroy Sterling's *My Sweet Lord*) were all second rate when compared to the JA versions put out on Trojan's labels. A lot of the JA material Pama were issuing was also

19

pretty lame, and there were even re-issues of older material being recycled. Even the tried and trusted supremos like Derrick Morgan and Owen Gray were doing mediocre medley versions of their old hits!

The upshot of all this is that Pama was now putting out more duffers than winners and seemed to have overreached itself at some point. The company collapsed early in '74 and Steve Bernard made an announcement to this effect to listeners of his *Reggae Time* radio show on BBC Radio London. Pama (or what was left of it) evolved into Jet Star Phonographics, which concentrated on distribution and is now run by the youngest Palmer brother, Carl.

Jet Star briefly resurrected Pama in 1975 for a short run of singles on the Pama, Bullet, Camel and (for one only) Punch labels, and a solitary LP which, judging by the illustration on the sleeve and some of the rather elderly tracks, was intended to be the next Pama album after *Straighten Up Volume 4* was issued in mid-'73.

Jet Star also issued some LPs and 12" 45s on the Pama label in the late Seventies by the likes of Tito Simon, The Marvels, Owen Gray and Derrick Morgan. Certainly, one or other of the Palmer Brothers was involved in producing a Tito Simon LP. There have been a couple of re-issues of Pama albums in recent years (the *Hot Numbers Volume 2* and *Reggae To Reggae* sets for example), but nobody seems to know whether Jet Star, like the present Trojan, has any sort of back catalogue it is willing or able to re-issue. To all intents and purposes though, Jet Star is primarily a distributor of other companies' records, but to this day there is still a record shop at 78 Craven Park Road, which must be some sort of record!

In addition to Trojan, Pama and the Doctor Bird Group, the only other major outlet for reggae during '69 was Bamboo. The label was set up in the summer of that year when Coxsone Dodd decided to establish new outlets for his productions to replace the Studio One and Coxsone labels now run by Trojan / B & C. He was apparently dissatisfied with the lack of promotion and publicity his labels were getting (and he was certainly having fewer successes than in '67-'68). Dodd gave over rights to his material to Junior Lincoln, a former sound system operator, who set up Bamboo as an exclusive outlet for Studio One product. The company struck paydirt with its first release around August '69 when Ken Parker's *My Whole World Is Falling Down* was a huge seller (in reggae terms anyway).

Bamboo set up its Banana subsidiary around the middle of 1970. By that time, Dodd's productions were "funkier" than before, fusing reggae with jazz and soul influences. This was also happening with other producers to a certain extent (such as Derrick Harriott's *Message From A Blackman* for example), but Dodd was doing a lot more of it. This "funky" reggae never really caught on with skinheads, and Bamboo and Banana were never really fully-fledged "skinhead" labels in the way that Trojan, Pama and the Doctor Bird Group were.

Bamboo's other subsidiary, Ackee, dealt with a multitude of producers and not just Dodd, and managed to release a few decent Dave Barker, Laurel Aitken and Owen Gray outings. Bamboo tended to issue a lot of "ethnic" product and only a handful of sides were given over to orchestral arrangements. Bamboo also issued some first-rate compilation albums which, unlike Trojan and Pama, often contained tracks which weren't issued as singles by the company.

By the end of '71, the company was releasing less product than before and not all of it was produced by Dodd either. Bamboo and Banana collapsed sometime in 1972, although Junior Lincoln continued to run Ackee and the fairly successful Ashanti label, a Bamboo offshoot started in '71. Trojan / B & C became involved in these two labels at a time when they too fell into financial difficulty. The company issued a few albums originally intended for release on Bamboo on its Attack subsidiary during 1974, together with a straight re-issue of John Holt's *A Love I Can Feel* set, one of Bamboo's biggest sellers. Lincoln was still active in the reggae business in '76 when he was running the Vulcan label.

By mid-'73, a number of other reggae labels were beginning to emerge just as Pama and Trojan were starting to lose their foothold in the market. With the collapse of Bamboo and the scrapping of some of the Trojan and Pama subsidiaries, there was plenty of room in the market for more reggae outlets. Shelly Music and Ethnic helped fill the gaps. The first was run by Count Shelly, one of London's foremost sound system operators. Beginning with its main Count Shelly label, it soon established Lord Koos, Penguin and Paradise as its subsidiaries. In '73, its major sellers were *No Potion A Gal* by Sang Hugh, *Break Up To Make Up* by Leroy Sibbles (but credited to Junior Byles on the label!), and a Bunny Lee recut of the Heptones' *Love Won't Come Easy*.

Ethnic was run by producer, record shop owner and one-time ska vocalist Larry Lawrence, and the label delivered the goods with his own *King Boxer* (under the name Duke Larry), *Rock Back* by The Selectors, Jimmy Stratdan's *So Long Baby*, and Dave Barker's reggae cover of *Stone In Love With You*. Many more "cottage industry" style labels continued to spring up during and after 1973 - Magnet, Faith, DIP and Black Wax to name but a few. Although nothing on these labels can be termed skinhead reggae, some of the material on the Count Shelly and Ethnic labels shouldn't be overlooked as it's definitely worth a listen. There were a number of worthwhile compilation LPs released on Count Shelley and Lord Koos which, frankly, put Trojan's efforts from that period firmly in the shade.

Unfortunately, it isn't easy to say exactly when West Indian sounds became the favoured music of skinheads. It is likely though that the *Club Ska* series was popular, largely because mods (who were the forerunners of skinheads) listened to ska back in their heyday of 1963-66. The other difficulty is that skinheads were probably part of a relatively small "underground" movement before April '69, when *Israelites* rocketed to the top of the charts. Certain discs, like Rudy Mills' *John Jones* and The Kingstonians' *Sufferer* had already been out for several months, but became firm skinhead favourites when the fans started checking out earlier reggae sounds. By 1970, the skinheads were big news everywhere.

Apart from Jamaican favourites such as Desmond Dekker, Derrick Morgan and The Maytals, Laurel Aitken was especially highly regarded by skinheads both as an artist and as a producer. His UK recorded sides on Pama's Nu-Beat subsidiary are all classics and sounded "basic" when compared to the JA material, as though they'd been recorded in the back room of some sweaty nightclub. Discs such as *Woppi King* and *Landlords And Tenants* were noticeably different from JA-produced reggae, although they also sold heavily to West Indian buyers as well as skinheads.

Joe Mansano, a long-time record shop owner in Brixton, turned his hand to production late in '68 with *Life On Reggae Planet* on Blue Cat. His material, such as Dice the Boss' *Brixton Cat* from '69, had a "shuffling" backbeat which became

POLL '69 AWARDS

FAVOURITE RECORDINGS

1. RETURN OF DJANGO: The Upsetters: Upsetter 301
2. WONDERFUL WORLD, WONDERFUL PEOPLE: Jimmy Cliff: Trojan 690
3. THE LIQUIDATOR: Harry J.'s All Stars: Trojan 675
4. THE ISRAELITES: Desmond Dekker: Pyramid
5. LONG SHOT (KICK THE BUCKET): The Pioneers: Trojan 672
6. WET DREAM: Max Romeo: Unity 503
7. HOW LONG WILL IT TAKE: Pat Kelley: Gas 115
8. WITHOUT YOU: Donnie Elbert: Deram 235
9. RED, RED WINE: Tony Tribe: Downtown 419
10. IT MEK: Desmond Dekker: Pyramid
11. LIVE INJECTION: Upsetters: Upsetter 313
12. REGGAE IN YOUR JEGGAE: Dandy: Downtown 410
13. MOON HOP: Derrick Morgan: Crab 32
14. POOR RAMESES: The Pioneers: Trojan 698
15. ELIZABETHAN REGGAE: Byron Lee/Boris Gardiner: Duke 39
16. SWAN LAKE: The Cats: BAF 1
17. PICKNEY GIRL: Desmond Dekker: Pyramid 6070
18. CUPID: Johnny Nash: Major Minor 603
19. HARD ROAD TO TRAVEL: Jimmy Cliff
20. SWEET SENSATION: The Melodians: Trojan 695

FAVOURITE ARTISTS

1. DESMOND DEKKER Pyramid
2. UPSETTERS Upsetter/Punch
3. JIMMY CLIFF Trojan
4. HARRY J's ALL STARS Harry J.
5. PIONEERS Trojan
6. JOHNNY NASH Major Minor
7. MAX ROMEO Unity
8. DONNIE ELBERT Deram
9. PAT KELLEY Gas
10. SYMARIP Treasure Isle
11. DANDY Downtown
12. DERRICK MORGAN Crab
13. LAUREL AITKEN Nu Beat
14. ETHIOPIANS
15. MAYTALS Trojan
16. MILLIE Pyramid
17. TONY TRIBE Downtown
18. PRINCE BUSTER Blue Beat
19. CATS Baf
20. BYRON LEE Duke

the trademark of UK skinhead reggae. More and more UK producers were emerging, and these homegrown sounds became hot property with both Pama and Trojan. Many however didn't cross over to the West Indian market, largely because they just never sounded like authentic JA product. So skinhead reggae was really made up of two strands - the JA material such as the tracks found on *Tighten Up Volume 2*, and the UK-produced stuff by the likes of Mansano, Dandy, Laurel Aitken and Lambert Briscoe. In-depth profiles of these men appear later.

Above: Reco Rodriguez, or Rico, was taught to play the trombone by the late great Don Drummond, but was originally a saxophonist.

The UK element of skinhead reggae started to die out towards the end of 1970 when the first wave of the cult began to peter out. By 1971, only Clancy Collins, Larry Lawrence, Sidney Crooks, and the threesome Webster Shrowder, Des Bryan, and Joe Sinclair (alias Bush Music), were still strong on the UK side of things. Trojan and Pama had both started to issue a fair amount of "roots" or rasta-influenced music which was not finding favour among skinheads or (later) suedeheads. Neither group were particularly interested in beating down Babylon, crossing the River Jordan or going back to Africa, and to cap it all the sounds weren't even as danceable as their predecessors.

Skinhead-suedehead interest was maintained for a time through the DJ, or "talkover" sounds of U Roy, I Roy, Dennis Alcapone and others. The DJ art has been covered extensively in other books and fanzines so I won't dwell on it too much here. The interest in the DJs had primarily started with King Stitt's *Fire Corner*, *Herbsman Shuffle* and *Vigorton 2* discs, and was in full swing when Dave and Ansel Collins' *Double Barrel* hit the UK number one spot in May '71. *Double Barrel* had in fact been issued in September '70, but, like *Israelites*, had taken months of exposure in the clubs, discos and dances before it made any headway on a national level. It was basically a prime example of a truly underground record which made the big time and was probably (with *Monkey Spanner*) among the last few real skinhead reggae records ever made.

By 1972, the DJs were the biggest news on the reggae scene. U Roy had done the business on a tour of the UK, and the stream of weekly releases by Dennis Alcapone, Winston Scotland, Lizzy, Big Youth, Prince Jazzbo and the like was extensive. The tunes were good (a lot of them were old Treasure Isle or Bunny Lee rhythm tracks which made them even better) and the lyrics didn't usually harp on about Haile Selassie. A lot of them were just plain good fun, like Dennis Alcapone's *Cassius Clay* or Scotty's *Skank In Bed*.

But all good things come to an end as they say, and the tide of black consciousness soon started showing through on DJ outings by Jah Stitch, Jah Woosh and Dillinger and the rhythms became much slower, echoing the sounds of the new dubwise music. By the close of '74, Big Youth and I Roy were the undisputed DJ kings, and the older hands like Alcapone and U Roy were having a hard time of it. A skinhead wouldn't know what the house of dreadlocks looked like even if it stared him in the face, and the DJ style had alienated what small white audience it had.

The only other area of the music that continued to attract the skinhead and suedehead faithful in the early Seventies was "rude" reggae. Judge Dread's series of discs on the "Big" theme (*Big Six*, *Big Seven*, etc. ,) were huge chart successes and, like Max Romeo's infamous *Wet Dream* from '69, sold massively without ever getting broadcast over the nation's airwaves. Charlie Ace And Fay's *Big Seven* also sold well to a white audience when issued in late '72.

The trend for this ribald music had started with calypso and, ironically, Chris Blackwell's

RIOT AT PIONEERS DANCE HALL DATE

THE PIONEERS, currently in our Reggae chart with "Poor Rameses" and the national hit, "Long Shot Kick The Bucket," figured in a major disturbance at Basildon Locarno on Friday, January 9. Pioneer Jackie Robinson was taken to the local hospital and treated for several cuts and shock but later released.

In all, 3 people were taken to hospital and 15 were arrested. One member of the backing group was arrested for possessing a weapon. Meanwhile, the group continue their tour with dates: University of Lancaster (Jan. 30), Hornsey Town Hall (Jan. 31), Bolero, Birmingham (Feb. 1), Alladice Hall, Brixton London (7), Civic Hall, St. Albans (14) and Tower Pier, Great Yarmouth (15).

24

first real taste of success came not with a ska disc but with Lord Kitchener's *Dr Kitch* calypso on Island's Jump Up subsidiary during 1963-64. This was one the black kids at school always brought to the end of term parties! There were sporadic forays into the rude side of things throughout the ska era (such as Jackie Opell's *More Wood* on Ska Beat and Justin Hinds' *Rub Up, Push Up* on Island) and rock steady (The Heptones' *Fat Girl* on Studio One and Phyllis Dillon's *Don't Touch Me Tomato* on Treasure Isle for instance). But when reggae arrived, the genre really came into its own.

Pama took maximum advantage of the demand for rude reggae sounds, putting out its *Bang Bang Lulu* compilation in '69. Max Romeo's mammoth *Wet*

Below: Judge Dread, real name Alex Hughes, had 11 national chart hits.

Dream ensured that Pama became something of a rude reggae specialist. Others followed on the label and its subsidiaries such as Lloyd Tyrell's (aka Charmers) *Birth Control* and *Mr Rhya*, Max Romeo's *Wine Her Goosie* and *Fish In The Pot,* and The Bleecher's *Ram You Hard*, which probably went further than anything else at the time in terms of blatant obscenity. The label's *Birth Control* compilation from 1970 is a classic set of rude reggae which is essential skinhead listening.

Prince Buster put out a fair amount of rude reggae at this time. He was an old hand at the game, having cut the excellent *Rough Rider* and *Wine And Grine* in '68. But apart from his classic *Big Five* single in '70, most of his later rude output was rather weak on rhythms and thin on ideas. His *Big Five* LP, which contained almost 100% rude tracks, tends to be quite tedious in fact, and represented the low point in his work (for me, Buster provided the best and - much later - worst in JA music). As a footnote, you may have noticed that Buster's name hasn't cropped up much so far in this book. This is largely because after '67-'68, he no longer held the dominant position he once did, given the arrival of new producers on the scene. He also seemed to excel at the early, fast type of reggae (such as on *Wine And Grine*), but found the going tough when the beat began to slow down.

On the UK side of things, rude reggae was particularly strong with naughty things from the likes of King Horror, Roy Smith, Trevor Lloyd, Girlie, Bim, Bam And Clover; and of course, the High Priest Of Reggae himself, Laurel Aitken. The skinheads lapped it up, but when their numbers started to decline so did the amount of rude reggae released, and by '72 there wasn't as much of it coming out.

That's where Judge Dread comes in. He started off something of a rude revival with his discs and inspired others to join in. Max Romeo did his thing again with *Pussy Watchman* on Pama; Fay And Matador had *Sex Grand National* out on Magnet; Henry And Liza did something called *Hole Under Crotches* on Dragon;

TOP 30 SINGLES

1	1	ELIZABETHAN REGGAE: Boris Gardiner: Duke 39 (5)
5	2	VIET NAM: Jimmy Cliff: Trojan 7722 (2)
2	3	SWEET SENSATION: The Melodians: Trojan 695 (5)
4	4	THE LIQUIDATOR: Harry J.'s All Stars: Trojan 675 (5)
9	5	SAMFIE MAN: The Pioneers: Trojan 7710 (2)
18	6	WITHOUT YOU: Donnie Elbert: Deram 235 (2)
6	7	PICKNEY GIRL: Desmond Dekker: Pyramid 6070 (5)
—	8	THE VAMPIRE: The Upsetters: Upsetter 317 (1)
10	9	CLINT EASTWOOD: The Upsetters: Punch 21 (3)
3	10	MOON HOP: Derrick Morgan: Crab 32 (5)
12	11	SKINHEAD MOON STOMP: Symarip: Treasure Isle 7050 (5)
14	12	POP A TOP: Andy Capp: Treasure Isle 7052 (5)
7	13	PRESSURE DROP: The Maytals: Trojan 7709 (4)
8	14	REGGAE PRESSURE: The Hippy Boys: High Note 035 (4)
15	15	LOCK JAW: Tommy & the Upsetters: Trojan 7717 (3)
—	16	BIRTH CONTROL: Lloyd Terrell: Pama 792 (1)
—	17	MONKEY MAN: The Maytals: Trojan 7711 (1)
24	18	GOT TO COME BACK: Delano Stewart: High Note 027 (4)
13	19	POOR RAMESES: The Pioneers: Trojan 698 (5)
26	20	BLACK COFFEE: Tommy McCook: Treasure Isle 7706 (2)
22	21	THE WARRIOR: The Sensations: Camel 31 (2)
29	22	COTTON DANDY: Ansell Collins: Trojan 7712 (2)
20	23	EASE UP: The Bleechers: Trojan 679 (3)
17	24	LEAVING ME STANDING: Winstone Groovey: Grape 3005 (2)
16	25	SHANGHAI: Freddie Notes & the Rudies: Trojan 7713 (3)
—	26	THE BULL: Freddie Notes & the Rudies: Duke 63 (1)
23	27	LET'S GO STEADY MY LOVE: Errol Daniels: MCA U.K. 5025 (3)
11	28	WONDERFUL WORLD, BEAUTIFUL PEOPLE: Jimmy Cliff: Trojan 690 (5)
—	29	THE BIG THREE: Harry J.'s All Stars: Harry J. 6601 (1)
21	30	MOONLIGHT GROOVER: Winston Wright: Trojan 7701 (3)

TOP 10 ALBUMS

1	1	TIGHTEN UP VOL. 2: Various Artists: Trojan TTL 7 (5)
2	2	RED, RED WINE: Various Artists: Trojan TTL 11 (5)
3	3	TIGHTEN UP VOL. 1: Various Artists: Trojan TTL 1 (5)
4	4	REGGAE POWER: Various Artists: Trojan TTL 10 (5)
9	5	FIRE CORNER: The Dynamites: Trojan TTL 21 (4)
5	6	THE UPSETTER: Various Artists: Trojan TTL 13 (5)
7	7	GUNS OF NAVARONE: Various Artists: Trojan TTL 16 (5)
—	8	REGGAE WITH BYRON LEE: Trojan TRLS 18 (1)
—	9	DANDY· YOUR MUSICAL DOCTOR: Trojan TTL 26 (1)
8	10	REGGAE SPECIAL: Various Artists: Coxsone 2 (5)

Nora Dean revived *Night Food Reggae* on Big Shot; and Lloydie And The Lowbites hit the top spot in the reggae charts in '74 with *Pussy Cat* on Harry J.

The formula began to wear thin very quickly however as a lot of the new rude reggae relied on Judge Dread style nursery rhyme patter. *Pussy Cat* was one such example and was a dreadful record. For anyone who doesn't know it, the song is half sung half spoken and features a guy asking another to guess the answer to a riddle which goes, "Dark like a dungeon, deep like a well, sweet like sugar and it nice no hell". The other guy keeps getting the answer wrong and so it goes on. If this was a Trojan best seller, the market's perception of good quality reggae must have changed a bit by 1974!

So that really wraps up where the skinhead interest in the music came in and where it ended. Although boots and braces skinheads were already thin on the ground by the dawn of 1972, there was still a white interest in reggae from those kids who were once skinheads but had mutated into suedeheads or "smooths", and from very young kids like myself who were beginning a lifelong interest in reggae.

THE PRODUCERS
From JA To The UK

The fields of ska, rock steady and reggae are almost unique in the popular music arena because the producer of a record is often considered to be as important as the actual artist who laid down the track. In Jamaica, the term "producer" also generally means "promoter" - that is the person who paid for the studio time (they usually owned the studio anyway) and paid the musicians and vocalists who played on the track. When the producer paid off the musicians, he also bought the exclusive rights to issue the track, and had in effect therefore bought the master tapes lock, stock and barrel. So the artist(s) received a one-off payment for their work - if the disc sold 500 copies or 50,000, he or she would never see another penny. Bob and Marcia never received a brass farthing beyond what producer Harry J gave them for *Young, Gifted and Black* despite it being a massive seller in the UK.

This was the way things worked in Jamaica, and if you've seen the film *The Harder They Come* you'll know what I'm talking about here. Royalties on sales were practically unheard of on the island - the producer scooped up the profits on discs sold, which was easy as they usually owned the labels the records were issued on!

The producers were then able to release "their" disc in JA and peddle it elsewhere. Trojan, Pama and other labels paid the producer for the rights to issue the track in the UK, and this would probably have been on the JA one-off payment basis as well rather than a "royalties" type arrangement. This system often failed when producers craftily sold their product to one or more different UK labels. To quote just one example, Derrick Morgan's *Seven Letters* (produced by Bunny Lee) appeared both on Pama's Crab and Trojan / B & C's Jackpot label when issued in 1969. It's easy to understand why the UK companies wanted to do their own

27

productions and so maintain exclusive rights to the material for their own respective labels. It was also probably cheaper as well.

So who were the major JA producers during the '67-'73 period? The "Big 13", in alphabetical order (ie in no particular order of importance or ranking) are described shortly. A lot has been written about some of them already in other publications (notably Coxsone Dodd, Duke Reid and Lee Perry) and so what follows are only short pen-pictures of each to give the uninitiated some background.

Coxsone Dodd

One of the earliest pioneers of the JA recording industry. Dodd was a major sound system operator on the island and began cutting his own acetates for exclusive airing at the dances and clubs. Most of the big names of the ska, rock steady and early reggae years recorded for him at one time or another - Delroy Wilson, The Wailers, The Heptones, Owen Gray, Alton Ellis, Slim Smith, The Maytals, the list is endless. Like Duke Reid however, his output began to dry up during the early Seventies, and he then began to concentrate his efforts on producing dub LPs using his classic Sixties Studio One rhythms.

Clancy Eccles

Eccles was initially a vocalist who cut a number of early ska sides for Coxsone Dodd in the late Fifties, notably *Freedom* and *River Jordan*, which came out over here on Blue Beat. He worked with a number of other producers until 1967, when he entered the production game himself. Skinhead-wise, his output on the Trojan / B & C subsidiary Clandisc between '69 and '70 is the most revered. His solo *Freedom* LP (Trojan TTL 22) is superb, as are his productions on King Stitt, Eric (Monty) Morris and his house band, The Dynamites. He seemed to drop out of the limelight after '73 and now focuses his energies on promoting his son's career.

Rupie Edwards

Initially a ska vocalist, Rupie Edwards came into the production game around 1968, releasing a number of sides on Doctor Bird in the UK. Pama issued a number of his discs over the next two years, and Dobby Dobson's *Strange* on Punch was a big success for him in '69. Trojan / B & C gave him their Big subsidiary the following year as an exclusive outlet for his music. Edwards really came into his own during the early Seventies with great sounds from The Gaylads, Errol Dunkley and Shorty The President. His own *Ire Feelings* on Cactus was a UK Top Ten hit in '74.

Joe Gibbs

Gibbs began selling records as a sideline to his TV repair business and had progressed to production by 1966. His first production was reputedly *Hold Them* by Roy Shirley (issued in the UK on Doctor Bird DB 1068), but by April 1968 his discs were coming out here on Island / B & C's Amalgamated label (later adopted by Trojan). This label was also the UK counterpart of Gibbs' JA outlet.

For skinheads, Amalgamated is one of the labels to collect, not least for the many Pioneers sides put out under their original name and their many aliases such as The Soulmates, The Slickers and The Reggae Boys. However, after the end of 1970 when Amalgamated was dropped by Trojan, the label's successor, Pressure Beat, was pale by comparison.

Derrick Harriott

Harriott had started out as part of the Jiving Juniors vocal group in the late Fifties, and was turning out solo discs by 1963, which initially tended to be in a slow soulful style rather than ska. He began his own Crystal and Move And Groove labels in JA around '67, and began to produce successful rock steady productions for himself (*Soloman*, *Walk The Streets* and *The Loser*), Keith And Tex (*Stop That Train* and *Tonight*), Rudy Mills (*Long Story*); and Lynn Tait And The Jets (*Something Stupid*). His earliest material was released in the UK on Island and included some superb, and now highly sought after, compilation and solo LPs.

Trojan / B & C gave him their Song Bird outlet for his UK releases in 1970, and he had further successes with the Crystalites' Spaghetti Western discs (more about them in chapter three), The Kingstonians, The Chosen Few, and his own *Message From A Blackman* and *Groovy Situation* 45s on the label. His early Seventies sides were in a more commercial vein however and were often covers of soul hits (such as on The Chi-Lites' *Have You Seen Her*). Harriott also produced DJ Scotty and a young Dennis Brown to great effect.

Harry J (Johnson)

Harry J's first major success was with The Beltones' *No More Heartaches*, issued here on Trojan (TR 628) in '68. He was particularly adept at the early reggae sound and Trojan's *No More Heartaches* compilation of his earliest productions provides the best introduction to his work. He became famous for Harry J All Stars' *Liquidator* (with Winston Wright on keyboards) and Bob and Marcia's *Young, Gifted And Black*, both of which were UK Top Ten hits on Trojan's Harry J subsidiary.

Leslie Kong

Kong had already been a producer for some six years before Desmond Dekker's *Israelites* took the world by storm. His '68 to '70 productions on Dekker, The Maytals, The Melodians and Ken Boothe display a bouncy type of reggae, heavy on bass and with very strong melodies. For some reason, his material is not that keenly collected today (except for his Bob Marley And The Wailers output), possibly because some of it (Ken Boothe's *Freedom Street* and the Jimmy Cliff and later Desmond Dekker sides for instance) are generally considered to be rather commercial.

Personally, I have always found Kong's productions to be among the very best of the peak reggae era. He was the one man able to make a reggae song cross over to a large section of the record-buying public without employing string sections and elaborate orchestrations (they were used on Jimmy Cliff's *Wonderful World, Beautiful People* at Cliff's insistence, not Kong's). He died in 1971, and many of the artists he produced never enjoyed success on a similar scale afterwards.

Bunny Lee

Lee was responsible for turning out some quite exceptional music between '67 and '73 by the likes of Slim Smith (with or without The Uniques), Pat Kelly, Delroy Wilson, John Holt, Derrick Morgan, Lester Sterling, Max Romeo and Dennis Alcapone. Island released his discs until 1969 when Trojan started to issue his material through its Jackpot subsidiary, and a whole host of his other productions came through Pama's Unity label. He was one of the first JA producers to issue "versions" of tried and tested rhythm tracks. For example, Max Romeo's *Wet Dream* was itself a version of Derrick Morgan's *Hold You Jack* and Lee later versioned it as *I Love You* (also by Derrick Morgan) and *Day Dream* by his house band, the Bunny Lee All Stars. If you see Lee's name on a label, you can't go far wrong.

Lee Perry

Perry is one of those producers you tend to either love or hate. However, the fast reggae sides Pama put out for him between '69 and '70 on their Camel and Punch subsidiaries by the likes of The Upsetters, The Inspirations, Busty Brown, Count Sticky and Dave Barker are undoubtedly skinhead reggae classics. Trojan's output on its Upsetter subsidiary tends to be quite patchy after '69, and much of it is in a slow "funky" reggae type vein. The *Clint Eastwood* compilation (Pama PSP 1014) is in my opinion one of the top ten skinhead reggae albums of all time. But on the other hand, Dave Barker's *Prisoner Of Love* album on Upsetter (TBL 127) is full of plodding, sparse reggae which is mind-numbingly boring. My advice is this: if you're able to, listen before you buy.

He started the cultural ball rolling earlier than most other producers with his Wailers, Junior Byles and Max Romeo material, but continued with some excellent DJ productions on Dennis Alcapone and I Roy. As the Seventies wore on however, Perry became weirder and he was one of the earliest exponents of dub.

Sonia Pottinger

About the only female producer in the business. Most of her UK output came through Doctor Bird and Island / B & C's High Note label (later adopted by Trojan). Her High Note output by The Hippy Boys, Delano Stewart, Delroy Wilson and Patsy is well worth having, although later stuff ('71-'72) was more pop oriented, and often consisted of covers of chart songs. Pottinger now owns exclusive rights to the late Duke Reid's productions and re-issues his material from time to time.

Prince Buster

Buster is a giant of the JA music business, both as a producer and as an artist. He, together with Coxsone Dodd and Duke Reid, dominated the industry until '68-'69 when some of the other names covered here happened along. His UK output was phenomenal - roughly 120 45s were issued under his name in the UK between 1961 and 1972, largely on Blue Beat. Production-wise, there were probably a few hundred. His *Al Capone* was a Top 20 hit in the UK in '67 and his tours here that year and three years earlier were also highly successful. As a ska artist, his reputation is unsurpassed and he can probably be regarded, together with Bob Marley, as the most renowned Jamaican musician of all time.

After the ska era had passed however, Buster had to struggle harder to retain his supremacy. His rock steady and reggae output was relatively small compared to his mammoth ska accomplishments, and by 1970 he was no longer such a big draw. In fact, things seemed to start going downhill soon after Blue Beat had folded to be succeeded by Melodisc's Fab subsidiary. Buster was never a particularly serious challenger to Coxsone and Duke Reid in the rock steady stakes, although his voice was quite well suited to the genre. His *She Was A Rough Rider* set on Fab is however a classic example of rock steady and early reggae.

Alvin Ranglin

Of all the producers mentioned so far, Ranglin has been written about the least. Trojan set up his GG subsidiary in 1970 but his earliest major successes came with The Maytones' *Sentimental Reason*, The GG All Stars' *Man From Carolina* and Verne And Son's *Little Boy Blue*. Some good stuff, some not so good.

Duke Reid

Reid's beginnings in the industry were similar to Dodd's, and the two men (along with Prince Buster) were to be main rivals throughout the duration of the ska, rock steady and early reggae eras. Reid's output on his Treasure Isle label between '67 and '68 featuring the many vocal harmony sides of (among others) The Techniques, The Paragons, The Melodians and Alton Ellis represents his real creative peak. Despite major success with U Roy material, Reid's output dropped in the early Seventies (as did Dodd's), possibly due to ill health. He died in 1974 after a long illness.

I must emphasise again that the foregoing outlines contain only the barest essentials of each producers' output (in fact, a complete book could and should be written covering the careers of reggae producers). Chris Prete wrote highly detailed articles on some of them in several of The Official Trojan Appreciation Society's fanzine, and due respect goes to Chris for his sterling work on these. However, it was necessary for me to say something about each of them to put chapter three in context. In JA music, producers are intrinsically linked to both the artist and the recording label concerned.

Among the many other producers worthy of mention are Winston Riley, Harry Mudie, JJ Johnson (alias Sir JJ), George Murphy, Lloyd Daley, Lloyd Charmers, Byron Smith, Herman Chin-Loy, and Phil Pratt.

The UK production scene consisted of just half a dozen or so men by '69. Some of them produced only a handful of sides, others were quite prolific, but for most of them their output was concentrated into just a couple of short years. A large amount of UK-produced reggae was laid down at Chalk Farm Studios near

Camden Town in London (Trojan certainly used this one a lot), and at a studio at the Club West Indies in Harlesden. Pama would have used this one for their UK produced material. But, unlike the JA scene, details on who produced what, where, and who played on it are practically non-existent, and the few people still in the business, like Reco Rodriguez (alias Rico) and Laurel Aitken, are the only sources of information. Acetates of discs are often a good indication of (at least) where a track was recorded, but they hardly exist for reggae. Anyway, here we go with the UK lot.

Laurel Aitken

Laurel, along with Reco Rodriguez and Owen Gray, was one of the earliest West Indian artists (he was in fact born in Cuba) to settle in the UK. Embarking on a singing career in 1951 as "El Cubano", he was at the forefront of the fledgling Jamaican recording industry in the mid to late Fifties, cutting a number of significant boogie and early ska sides for Duke Reid such as *Judgement Day*, *Railroad Track*, *More Whisky* and *Mighty Redeemer*, and Ken Khouri (for *Bartender*). These sides were put out on Melodisc's Blue Beat label in the UK, probably several years after they first appeared in JA. His output on Esquire's Starlite label, such as *Little Sheila*, *Love Me Baby* and *Drinking Whisky*, also enjoyed healthy sales via the West Indian immigrant population (rumour has it that *Little Sheila* was in fact the first early ska recording to be issued here, probably around the middle of 1960).

By mid-'61, some of his Blue Beat sides were being produced in the UK (probably by Laurel himself) and he soon became an integral part of the UK ska scene. Island however also began issuing discs under his name produced in JA (by Leslie Kong), so no doubt he was keeping his irons in both fires so to speak. By 1964, his discs were being recorded and issued in the UK by Rita and Benny King's R & B label, Blue Beat, Dice (another Melodisc subsidiary) and Rio.

His style was never particularly suited to the rock steady idiom, but the dawn of early reggae and the

Man who started it all . . .

LAUREL AITKEN: first

SPARE a thought, as the day of the Caribbean Music Festival draws near, for the man who claims to have started the whole thing, both here and in Jamaica . . . Laurel Aitken.

Laurel's been resident in Britain since 1960, has made well over 100 singles, and to those who know, is the one man who really knows how to sing bluebeat with that authentic touch!

"My first record in Jamaica was called 'Little Sheila'—we called it ska over there, and it was the very first record of this kind of music ever released. Before that it was all calypsos. I just took the calypso style guitar, slightly changed the way of playing it and mixed in a little jazz, and out came this new rhythm. That was at least five years before Prince Buster, who's often thought of as being the first ska singer.

"I came to Britain in 1960 and made a record for Melodisc called 'Mary Lee'—and that was the first time people in Britain had ever heard bluebeat."

Laurel confirms that as far as home-grown blue-

beat was concerned, the first man to give it a try was our old mate Georgie Fame.

In the early days Laurel found he was preaching to the converted by playing only to West Indian immigrants.

"In fact it wasn't until about two years ago that British teenagers started taking an interest in ska—or rock steady as it was by then."

Laurel still works regularly around clubs in the Midlands, as well as producing singles for Pama Records—one of the many new all-bluebeat labels—and pins high hopes on his next single "Don't Be Cruel," the old Elvis Presley song.

REGGAE
TOP 30

1 TR 695	Sweet Sensation	Melodians
2 TR 7710	Samfie Man	Pioneers
3 DU 39	Elizabethan Reggae	Byron Lee
4 PYR 6078	Pickney Gal	Desmond Dekker
5 TR 698	Poor Rameses	Pioneers
6 TI 7052	Pop a Top	Andy Capp
7 HS 027	Got to Come Back	Delano Stewart
8 TR 7709	Pressure Drop	Maytals
9 TR 690	Wonderful World, Beautiful People	Jimmy Cliff
10 TR 675	Liquidator	Harry J. All Stars
11 TI 7050	Skinhead Moon Stomp	Symarip
12 HS 035	Reggae Pressure	Hippy Boys
13 TR 7717	Lock Jaw	Tommy & The Upsetters
14 TR 679	Ease Up	Bleechers
15 TR 7712	Cotton Dandy	Ansell Collins
16 EX 2005	Bombshell	Crystalites
17 GR 3005	Leaving Me Standing	Winston Groovey
18 TR 7706	Black Coffee	Tommy McCook
19 CLA 201	Dollar Train	Clancy Eccles
20 TR 7704	Dry Up Your Tears	Bruce Ruffin
21 US 324	Yakety Yak	Lee Perry & The Upsetters
22 AMG 855	Nevada Joe	Joe Gibb & The Destroyers
23 CLA 206	The Ugly One	King Stitt
24 TR 7713	Shanghai	Freddie Notes & The Rudies
25 US 313	Live Injection	Upsetters
26 DU 50	Brixton Cat	Joe's All Stars
27 US 301	Return of Django	Upsetters
28 TR 7722	Vietnam	Jimmy Cliff
29 GR 3011	Babylon Burning	Freddie Notes & The Rudies
30 TR 658	Fattie Fattie	Clancy Eccles

TROJAN

creation of Pama's Nu-Beat subsidiary changed all that. For a time, it became very much "his" label, and his skills as a producer were much in demand by both Pama and Trojan. His list of production credits is extensive in UK terms - Pama Dice, Dice the Boss, King Horror, Winston Groov(e)y, Trevor Lloyd, Tiger, The Versatiles, and The Classics (UK) to name but a few. Together with his own discs, Laurel represented UK skinhead reggae at its best from '69 to '70. Not surprisingly then, a lot of his output is listed in chapter three.

By the latter part of 1970, his own records were in a very commercial style and were mostly love songs. His *It's Too Late (To Say That You're Sorry)* on Trojan (TR 7826) from '71 was very nearly a national hit. Later in the Seventies, he recorded on and off for several labels but remained relatively quiet until the Two Tone craze when he was again very much in demand.

Lambert Briscoe

Briscoe ran his own Hot Rod sound system in Brixton and helped set up the Torpedo label with Eddy Grant of The Equals. His Torpedo sides were usually very skinhead-flavoured - *Pussy Got Nine Life*, *Skinhead Moondust*, *Moon Hop In London* and *Skinheads Don't Fear* were all issued under the banner of The Hot Rod All Stars. Most of them were in fact pretty good and were among the better UK-produced skinhead reggae records of the period. Trojan must have liked his material as they gave him his own Hot Rod outlet after issuing several sides on both Duke and Trojan itself. After Trojan dropped Hot Rod from its roster towards the end of 1970, Briscoe appeared to have aborted his production career.

Nat Cole

Nat was the proprietor of an afro-wig store in Brixton's Atlantic Road and produced a handful of sides during 1970. His own *Sugar Sugar* on Jackpot (JP 722) and Rita Alston's *Popcorn Funky Reggae* on Trojan (TR 7751) are the best known, and both did well enough to justify an appearance on Trojan's *Reggae, Reggae, Reggae* (TBL 130) and *Funky Chicken* (TBL 137) compilations respectively. However, after a couple of mediocre things on Creole he appeared to have gone back to his main business of selling wigs.

Clancy Collins

Clancy, or "Sir Collins" as he was also known, started his own Collins Down Beat label in the UK towards the end of 1967. This utilised his own productions as well as some Bunny Lee material. This label shut up shop in '68 and Collins put out some sides on Island / B & C's Blue Cat and Duke labels over the next year or so, and some good sides on Ackee in '71 (like Owen Gray's *Whispering Bells* for instance). He began another self-run label around '73, Collins Music Wheel, which featured a lot of material from his sons and daughters (they were a truly musical family) and a dub LP or two later in the Seventies. After an LP tribute to those who perished in the New Cross fire in '81 (his son Steve was one of those who died that night) Sir Collins, like many of the other UK production men listed here, seems to have disappeared from the reggae world.

Sidney Crooks

Along with George Agard (Desmond Dekker's half-brother) and Jackie Robinson, Sid was one third of The Pioneers. Having settled in the UK following the success of *Long Shot Kick The Bucket*, his earliest known productions were on Pama's Bullet label with *Return Of Batman* (BU 436) and *Outer Space* (BU 437), both credited to Sidney's All Stars. He had a rather annoying habit of using names of Jamaican outfits on his discs, like The Slickers (formerly a Pioneers pseudonym) and The Viceroys, who sounded nothing like their JA counterparts! He was still producing for Trojan in the late Seventies and now operates his own studio.

Dandy (Livingstone)

Dandy (real name Robert Thompson) settled in the UK in 1959 and later began working in a record shop run by Lee Gopthal housed in the same premises as Island and the Planetone recording studio in Kilburn Park's Cambridge Road. He cut a few sides with a vocal group called The Keynotes for Planetone and heard via Gopthal that a new label, Carnival, was looking for a Jamaican duo to make UK ska recordings. He subsequently teamed up with Sugar Simone (aka Les Foster, Keith Foster, Lance Hannibal, Calva L Foster and Tito Simon at various times!) to become one half of Sugar And Dandy.

Their *Let's Ska* and *Time And Tide* were very successful for Carnival, the latter reputedly selling some 25,000 copies. Later discs weren't as big however, and after Carnival folded in 1965, Dandy parted company with Sugar Simone and recorded for the Ska Beat label, which was part of Rita and Benny King's R & B empire. He had a big seller on Ska Beat with *Rudy, A Message To You* in '67, and this prompted R & B to set up Giant as a further subsidiary designed to issue almost 100% Dandy product. It was on this label that Dandy got his first real taste of production work on sides by Don Martin (his *Keep On Fighting* is a classic), Herbie Gray, Jeanette Simpson and his own backing band, The Superboys.

Having built up an impressive stable on Giant and with a big seller on Trojan with *Donkey Returns* (credited to The Brother Dan All Stars), Dandy received an offer he couldn't refuse when old friend Lee Gopthal gave him Down Town as an exclusive outlet for his productions when Trojan / B & C was set up.

Down Town's first 45, Dandy's own *Move Your Mule*, was a blinding piece of early reggae from late '68 and was followed by *Tell Me Darling*, *I'm Your Puppet* and *Reggae In Your Jeggae* - a consistent run of superb skinhead reggae sides. His productions on Tony Tribe, Desmond Riley, The Israelites, Reco (with whom he cut an entire LP), The Rudies, Sonny Binns, and The Music Doctors (Down Town's house band) are also worthy of much praise. Both the Reco LP (entitled *Blow Your Horn* on TTL 11) and the first volume of Trojan's *Red Red Wine* compilation (TTL 12) enjoyed healthy sales. Trojan gave Dandy another exclusive outlet - the J-Dan label early on in 1970.

Things started going off the boil a bit when Dandy began putting out slow soul material on Down Town, usually dueting with a young sweet-voiced singer called Audrey. A couple of entire LPs were given over to this type of thing (*I Need You* and *Morning Side Of The Mountain*) and both should be avoided at all costs if you're not into this type of music. Dandy may have been attempting to revive the "Jackie And Millie" spirit for late Sixties consumption, but must have failed miserably as these discs were (deservedly) poor sellers alongside the real reggae stuff.

By the closing months of 1970, a fair chunk of Down Town and J-Dan's output had become pretty mediocre, and a Music Doctors' instrumental LP entitled *Reggae In The Summertime* (aka *Carry On Doctor*) had not done as well as Dandy's earlier *Musical Doctor* album. The two labels were releasing a great deal of material but little of it was doing much business. Apart from Boy Friday's excellent *Version Girl* on Down Town, only a reggae cover of *In The Summertime* and a stepping piano-led instrumental entitled *Bush Doctor* (both by the Music Doctors and both on J-Dan) were big reggae hits for him during this particular time.

Having become disillusioned by his lack of commercial success, both as a producer and artist, Dandy returned to Jamaica to seek new-found inspiration. This he ultimately found, and his own *Suzanne Beware Of The Devil* was a Top 20 hit late in '72, followed by a further Top 30 disc with the double A sider *Big City* / *Think About That*, both on Trojan's Horse subsidiary (J-Dan had by then been scrapped and Down Town began to focus on productions from JA). Success was short and sweet however and by 1974 he was back in the doldrums. After a US LP in '77, he seems to have disappeared from the public eye completely.

Les Foster

I have already mentioned Foster, and his many aliases, in the Dandy profile. He appeared to produce very little and only three notable discs have come to my attention - his own *Run Like A Thief* on Torpedo, The Saints' *Windy* on Big Shot, and Roy Smith's rude *See Through Craze* on Grape (as "Calva L Foster"). It's a pity he didn't do more as these are all well above par for UK stuff and worth picking up if you come across them.

Larry Lawrence

Lawrence was originally a ska vocalist in the early Sixties whose *Garden of Eden* was released here on Island in '63. He began producing in the UK during

Opposite page: Dandy Livingstone (photo by Barry Plummer)

1970 and cut some sides for the Jackpot label by the likes of McBean Scott and Errol And The Champions as well as himself. These sides are so rare however that I have never come across them.

A year or so later, he did some stuff for Duke, and The Sensations' reggae cover of Dawn's *What Are You Doing Sunday* from '71 was quite successful for him on this label. Otherwise, he produced a number of sides on Bamboo's Banana and Ackee subsidiaries. He soon opened his own record shop in Brixton and started the Ethnic label around 1973, whereupon his production career really began to get off the ground with Sydney Rodgers' classic *Miracle Worker* and King Tapper (Zukie)'s *Jump And Twist*. He introduced the Fight label as a sister label to Ethnic in '74. Ethnic was still around in the late Seventies and early Eighties, but I've no idea whether Lawrence is still involved in the music business today.

Joe Mansano

Mansano was the proprietor of Joe's Record Shack in Granville Arcade, Brixton Market. He was one of the first West Indians to start selling records in the area, having started his first outlet in the market in the early Sixties. His production on Reco's *The Bullet* on Blue Cat in May '69 was successful enough to prompt Trojan to issue some of his work on its Joe label, which shared the Duke label's existing numbering system rather than having its own. His studio band, Joe's All Stars, had some quite popular discs out on Joe at the time, including a reggae cover of *Hey Jude*.

His series of Dice The Boss sides on Joe, including *Brixton Cat*, *Gun The Man Down* and *Your Boss DJ*, found favour with black buyers as well as white. In fact, Mansano's output must have impressed Trojan sufficiently for them to issue their *Brixton Cat* compilation LP of his productions, which has become one of the most popular skinhead reggae albums of all time. Trojan had by 1970 also established the Joe label as a separate entity from Duke, with its own numbering system. In addition to the Joe label releases, Mansano was producing good skinhead-flavoured material on Reggae, a short-lived label set up that year by Graeme Goodall of the Doctor Bird Group.

By the end of 1970 Trojan had dropped the Joe label, probably because sales had been falling as the skinheads declined in numbers. It's also fair to say that the Mansano production formula had begun to wear a bit thin. The Reggae label had also folded, giving him no UK outlets. In '72 however, President's Sioux label bought some of his back catalogue and re-issued a few of his best sellers, possibly because they were still popular in suedehead circles.

Mansano started his own Arrow label in mid-'73 with Ray Martell, who cut the classic *She Caught The Train* for the Joe label (later reissued on Sioux). Most of Arrow's output was very middle-of-the-road and is of absolutely no interest to skinheads. Mansano's shop was still in operation by 1987 but has closed down since then. His current whereabouts aren't known, although he probably sold up and returned to JA for good. I know a few people in the fanzine business who'd like an interview with him though.

J Sinclair

Sinclair's main claim to fame was the tracks he produced for Freddie Notes And The Rudies for various Trojan subsidiaries between '69 and '70. After Notes and Co. had metamorphosed into the pop-reggae group Greyhound in early '71, Sinclair teamed up with Webster Shrowder and Des Bryan to form Bush Music. Most of Bush's formative productions were on Trojan's revived Black Swan subsidiary, and The Lowbites' *I Got It*, and Selwyn Baptiste's instrumental version of *Montego Bay* (in fact titled *Mo' Bay*) were popular discs on the label. Bunny Lee was also associated with Bush for a time.

The Bush team built up quite an empire with names like The Stags, The Deltones, The Swans and Paddy Corea, and much of their material can be found on the three volumes of Trojan's *Music House* compilation albums.

Apart from those mentioned above, other producers doing the rounds in the UK included Bruce Anthony, Nehemia Reid, Count Suckle and Derrick Morgan who laid down a number of tracks while resident here.

SIOUX RECORDS Ltd.
(Distributed by President Records Limited)
Kassner House,
1 Westbourne Gardens,
London, W2 5NR

SINGLE RELEASES

SI 013	**POOCH JACKSON** YOU JUST GOTTA GET READY **BROTHER DAN** DJANGO'S VALLEY
SI 014	**JOE HIGGS** THE WAVE OF WAR **JUMBO STERLING** SHAFT
SI 015	**JACKIE ROWLAND** INDIAN RESERVATION **JUNIOR SMITH** I'M IN A DANCING MOOD
SI 016	**POOCH JACKSON** with The Harry J. Allstars **ONCE BITTEN** **KING REGGIE** SLAVE DRIVER

The above records are available from:
ALL SELECTA DEPOTS.
President Van Sales.
H. R. Taylor, (Birmingham) Ltd., 139 Bromsgrove Street, Birmingham 5.
Solomon & Peres, Belfast & Dublin.
Clyde Factors (Electrical) Ltd., 79, Washington Street, Glasgow, C.3.
Lugton's Ltd., 209-212, Tottenham Court Road, London, W.1.
E.M.I. (Ireland) Limited, 23 Lower Dominick Street, Dublin 1.
All Exports: E.M.I. Limited, E.M.I. House, 20, Manchester Square, W.1.

CHAPTER TWO
LIST OF UK LABELS ISSUING JAMAICAN MUSIC (1959-73)

One of the things that has never (to my knowledge anyway) been put into print is a definitive list of all the record labels which issued Jamaican music in the UK during the ska, rock steady and early reggae years. After a great deal of research spanning several years, I've come up with the following 139. Although many of them will be well known to a lot of you out there, the list does cover ones which are very rarely seen these days. It isn't an exclusively "skinhead reggae" list, but aims to cover practically anything a Jamaican music collector (of whatever sort) might be interested in. One of the reasons for such a large coverage is because ska, rock steady and reggae labels often contain no reference to the year of issue. When I came across a dealer recently describing an undated Count Shelly label 45 as "rare late Sixties" (with a price tag to match), I decided that collectors really needed to have as much information at their disposal as possible.

I've used the term "Jamaican music" quite loosely as some of them released calypso, gospel, mento, hi-life or Guyanese music (or just plain crap). At least they should give an indication of musical content and a guide to what and what not to buy should you come across them at record fairs and the like. Some of them, like the President labels, didn't specialise in Jamaican music, but put out a run of skinhead reggae titles by The Pyramids under various guises. Most of the major UK record companies dabbled in reggae at one time or another (like CBS for instance who issued a Bob Marley single in '72), but unless they set up dedicated subsidiary labels or released a reasonable amount of the music, I've omitted them from the list.

After each label name comes the name of the owner / distributor and the known date(s) of operation. There are several labels with question marks after them as I frankly have no information about them whatsoever! Also, although I know that some of the later labels (like Cactus and Magnet for example) were started in a certain year, I don't necessarily know when they stopped. I've therefore had to resort to a "best guesstimate" on these. Now read on . . .

1. Ackee (Bamboo / Junior Lincoln '69-'72 and Trojan / B&C '73-'75)
2. Airborne (? '66: only two soul releases by JA artists)
3. Aladdin (Island '65: mostly slow soul from the likes of Owen Gray and Jackie Edwards)
4. Amalgamated (Island / B&C and Trojan / B&C '68-'70: also issued a short-lived gospel series)
5. Amusicon (? '67: possibly just the one issue by Dave Smith And The Astronauts, which also came out on Columbia Blue Beat)
6. Arrow (Joe Mansano '73-'77)
7. Ashanti (Bamboo '71-'72 and Trojan / B&C '73-'75)

8. Atra (Brent Clark / Atra Records & Music Ltd '73-'75)
9. Attack (Doctor Bird Group '69 and Trojan / B&C '70-'78)
10. BAF (BAF Records / Tranco Ltd '68-'70)
11. Bamboo (Junior Lincoln '69-'72: a few albums with Bamboo catalogue numbers went out on the Attack label during '74)
12. Bamboo Now (Junior Lincoln / Bamboo '71: one issue only)

13. Banana (Junior Lincoln / Bamboo '70-'72)
14. Big (Trojan / B&C '70-'73)6
15. Big Shot (Island / B&C and Trojan / B&C '68-'75)
16. Black Swan (Island '63-'65 and Trojan / B&C '70-'71)
17. Blue Beat (Melodisc '60-'67)
18. Blue Cat (Island / B&C and Trojan / B&C '68-'69)
19. Blue Mountain (Island '71-'73)
20. Bread (Trojan / B&C '70-'73)
21. Bullet (Pama '69-'73 first series and '75 second series)
22. Cactus (Creole Records '72-'78)
23. Caltone (R & B Discs '67-'68)
24. Camel (Pama '69-'73 first series and '75 second series)
25. Caribou (R & B Discs '65)
26. Carnival (Crossbow '63-'65: a few issues were of a pop, soul and jazz nature and some of the label's output was re-issued on the Page One label in '67)
27. Chek (? '62)
28. Clandisc (Trojan / B&C '69-'72)
29. Collins Down Beat (Clancy Collins '67-'68)
30. Collins Music Wheel (Clancy Collins '73-'81)
31. Columbia Blue Beat (EMI '67-'70)
32. Count Shelly (Shelly Music '72-'76)
33. Coxsone (Island / B&C and Trojan / B&C '67-'69)
34. Crab (Pama '68-'71)
35. Creole (Trojan / B&C '70-'71, but later independent)
36. Crystal (Ed Kassner / President '69-'75)
37. Dice (Melodisc '62-'66 first series and '69 second series: one issue only)
38. Dinosaur (Creole Records / Jaguar '73)
39. Direct (Doctor Bird Group '66-'67)
40. Doctor Bird (Doctor Bird Group '66-'69 first series and Trojan / B&C '70 second series)

41. Double D (? '67-'68: also issued a gospel series using identical labels)
42. Down Town (Trojan / B&C '68-'73)
43. Dragon (Island '73 and Trojan / B&C '73-'75)
44. Duke (Melodisc '60-'61)
45. Duke (Island / B&C and Trojan / B&C '68-'73)
46. Duke Reid (Trojan / B&C '70-'73)
47. Dynamic (Trojan / B&C '70-'72 and Creole '76-'78)
48. Escort (Pama '69-'71)
49. Ethnic (Larry Lawrence '73-'77: initially a Creole Records label)
50. Explosion (Trojan / B&C '69-'74)
51. Fab (Melodisc '66-'72)
52. Gas (Pama '68-'71)
53. Gayfeet (Trojan / B&C '69-'70 first series and '73 second series)
54. GG (Trojan / B&C '70-'73)
55. Giant (R & B Discs '67-'68: also issued an African music series using identical labels)
56. Grape (Trojan / B&C '69-'73: no issues in '71)
57. Green Door (Trojan / B&C '71-'74)
58. Hala-Gala (Hala Gala Music and Films '65-69: mainly Guyanese/South American music)
59. Harry J (Trojan / B&C '69-'74: early releases used Trojan catalogue numbers)
60. High Note (Island / B&C and Trojan / B&C '68-'74)
61. Hillcrest (R & B Discs '71-'72)
62. Hornet (Melodisc '62)
63. Horse (Trojan / B&C '71-'78)
64. Hot Lead (? '72-'74)
65. Hot Rod (Trojan / B&C '70)
66. Hot Shot (Torpedo '70)
67. Island (Island '62-'68)
68. Jackpot (Trojan / B&C '69-'73)
69. Jaguar (? '73-'74)
70. Jay Boy (Ed Kassner / President '69: a few reggae issues only)
71. J-Dan (Trojan / B&C '70-'71)

72. JJ (Doctor Bird Group '68-'70: not actually a label in its own right since its releases used Doctor Bird and Pyramid catalogue numbers. It got its own JJ prefix in 1970, but the output from this year was largely re-issued material from the earlier imprint)
73. J.N.A.C. (R & B Discs: one calypso issue only)
74. Joe (Trojan / B&C: earlier releases used Duke catalogue numbers)
75. Jolly (R & B Discs '68-'69: Dandy's *Rudy, A Message To You* also appeared on this label with its Ska Beat catalogue number)

76. Jump-up (Island '62-'64 and Trojan / B&C '71: an all calypso label)
77. Junior (Junior Lincoln '69-'71)
78. Kalypso (Melodisc '61-'63: mostly calypso and mento)
79. King (R & B Discs '65: only a few JA music releases)
80. Limbo (Melodisc '60)
81. London (reggae series) (Decca '70-'72)
82. Lord Koos (Shelly Music '73-'76)
83. Magnet (Magnet Records '73-'76: another Magnet label existed at the same time focusing on pop and soul music)
84. Mary Lyn (Revolution '69-'70)
85. Master Time (Doctor Bird Group '68: most issues were gospel numbers done in rock steady style)
86. Melodisc (Melodisc '59-'61: mostly calypso, pop, boogie, etc., but an early Laurel Aitken release as well)
87. Melody (Melodisc '68)
88. Moodisc (Trojan / B&C '70-'72 and R & B Discs '72-'75)
89. National Calypso (R & B Discs '64: two issues only)
90. Nu-Beat / Newbeat (Pama '68-'71: despite the subtle name change, essentially one and the same label)
91. Ocean (Pama '70 first series, '72 - one issue only - and '75 second series)
92. Pama (Pama '67-'73 first series: many soul releases, and '75 (2nd series)
93. Pama Supreme (Pama '70-'74)
94. Planetone (Sonny Roberts '62-'64)
95. Port-o-Jam (R & B Discs '64)
96. President (Ed Kassner '67-'69: a long-running pop and soul label, but only a few rock steady and reggae releases in the late Sixties)
97. Pressure Beat (Trojan / B&C '70-'73)
98. Prince Buster (Melodisc '70-'72)
99. Punch (Pama '69-'72 and a one-off issue in '75)
100. Pyramid (Doctor Bird Group '67-'69 and Trojan / B&C '73-'74)
101. Q (Trojan / B&C '70)
102. R & B (R & B Discs '63-'64)
103. Rainbow (Melodisc '66-'67)

104. Randy's (Trojan / B&C '70-'73)
105. Reggae (Doctor Bird Group '69-'70: another label under this name was issued by Creole Records later in the Seventies)
106. Revolution Rock Steady and Reggae series (Immediate '68-'69 and D & H Productions '70)
107. Rhino (EMI / Creole Music '72-'74)
108. Rio (Graeme Goodall / Doctor Bird Group '63-'67)
109. Rude Boy (Hala-Gala Music And Films '69)
110. Rymska (? '66)
111. Shades (Ian Smith '71)

STARLIGHT ROOMS BOSTON TEL: 3579

SAT.
SEPT. 20 **DESMOND DEKKER**

Bars–Refreshments–Meals–Dancing 7-12   10/-

---

112. Silver (? ?: possibly just the one issue, by Silver And The Magnets, one half of which was also put out on the Jolly label)
113. Sioux (Ed Kassner / President '72-'73)
114. Ska Beat (R & B Discs '64-'67: this was actually a continuation of the R & B label which became an outlet for non-ska material only and adopted a new catalogue prefix (MRB). It follows that Ska Beat adopted R & B's original JB prefix)
115. Smash (Trojan / B&C '70-'73)
116. Song Bird (Trojan / B&C '69-'73)
117. Soulfood (? ?, 1973)
118. Sound of Jamaica (Clancy Collins '68: one issue only using Collins Down Beat label catalogue number)
119. Sound System (R & B Discs '69)
120. Spinning Wheel (Trojan / B&C '70-'71)
121. Spur (Creole Records '71-'72)
122. Star (Melodisc '69)
123. Starlite (Esquire Records '60-'61)
124. Studio One (Island / B&C and Trojan / B&C '67-'69)
125. Success (Pama '69-'70)
126. Sugar (Decca '70)
127. Supreme (Pama '69-'71: another label by this name was issued by a different company in the mid-Seventies)
128. Summit (Trojan / B&C '70-'73)
129. Sway (Sonny Roberts / Planetone '63)
130. Techniques (Trojan / B&C '70-'74)

131. Torpedo (Lambert Briscoe / Eddy Grant '70 first series and '75 second series)
132. Treasure Isle (Island '67-'68, Doctor Bird Group '69 and Trojan / B&C '71-'73)
133. Trojan (Island / B&C and Trojan / B&C '67-'85)
134. Tropical (Bamboo '71-'72: later taken over by Creole)
135. Unity (Pama '68-'71 and a one-off issue in '73)
136. Up-front (Beacon (?) '69-'70)
137. Upsetter (Trojan/B&C '69-'73)
138. Venus (Doctor Bird Group '65: slow soul from Owen Gray and Laurel Aitken)
139. Wirl (Doctor Bird Group '66-'67: actually used Doctor Bird catalogue numbers)

Caribbean Music Festival

"IN REGGAE TIME"

EMPIRE POOL, WEMBLEY

SUNDAY, 21st SEPTEMBER, 1969
6 p.m. — 10.30 p.m.

★ STAR APPEARANCES BY ★

JOHNNY NASH
DESMOND DEKKER
MAX ROMEO JIMMY CLIFF
JACKIE EDWARDS
JIMMY JAMES

COUNT PRINCE MILLER : TONY TRIBE
ROOT & JENNY JACKSON
BLACK VELVET : DEREK MORGAN
MOHAWKS : PAT KELLY : SKATALITES

Compered by (Mr. B.B.C. himself) DWIGHT WHYLIE

and (Caribbean's No. 1 Entertainer)
COUNT PRINCE MILLER

Doors open at 5 o'clock. Festival starts at 7 o'clock. Licensed Bars, Restaurants, Fun Stalls, Cafeteria, Snacks, Record Stalls.
Underground to Wembley Park or appropriate Buses.

10/-   16/-   20/-   24/-   30/-

Tickets in advance purchased from:
THE BOX OFFICE, EMPIRE POOL, WEMBLEY; RECORDS & MUSIC, 52 Stoke Newington Road, N.16; HARRINGAY RECORDS LTD., 73 Grand Parade, N.4; DEREK'S RECORDS, 5 Turnpike Lane, N.8; AERO ELECTRICS, 108 Acton Lane, N.W.10; PADDINGTON TRANSPORT, 6 Great Western Road, W.9; JOE'S RECORD SHOP, 93 Granville Arcade, Atlantic Road, S.W.9; HARVEYS, 276 Green Street, Forest Gate, E.7.
TICKETS AVAILABLE ONLY AT ABOVE ADDRESSES OR TEL: BOX OFFICE, WEMBLEY 902 1234 TO RESERVE YOUR SEAT AND TICKET.

Promoted by The Round Table of Wimbledon Charity Organisation

During early 1973, a company called Mooncrest became involved with Trojan / B&C, and was one of several pop labels distributed by B&C. I'm not exactly sure where they fitted into the picture, but I've not mentioned them in the above list or elsewhere in this book so as to avoid confusion.

CHAPTER THREE
BOSS SOUNDS
Classic Skinhead Reggae

As you'll have seen from chapter two, there were just so many labels issuing ska, rock steady and reggae in the UK that the potential punter is often left confused about what to buy and what to avoid. This chapter will concentrate on the quality and quantity of skinhead reggae and rock steady released on UK labels between '67 and '73. An A-Z of the labels follows which takes account of roughly two-thirds of those listed in chapter two. Those I've omitted released ska (which falls outside the main remit of this book) or later reggae and other types of music which probably won't be of interest to the average skin.

From first-hand experience, I know that a lot of collectors of Jamaican music tend to buy records based on the labels, the artist or the producer without ever having heard them (I've done this myself plenty of times). For instance, I remember buying a single, *My Girl*, by the Ethiopians on Duke a few years ago on the assumption that, if it was by The Ethiopians, it must be a sure-fire belter. I was proved wrong when it turned out to be a slow soul track. To give another example, Pama's Crab subsidiary has always been of special interest to skinheads, but the good quality music (even the Derrick Morgan cuts) really starts to peter out towards the end of the series. So buying records on the basis of label, artist or producer alone can be a pretty risky business. I hope the following at least steers you in the right direction.

Following each label profile is a list of what are, in my view, the best skinhead reggae singles released between 1967 and 1973 on a cross-section of UK labels (ie a large chunk of those listed in two). Again, I've used the term "skinhead reggae" quite loosely since the late ska and rock steady releases listed would certainly appeal to a lot of skins.

Any personal selection is obviously bound to be highly subjective. Where this one differs from earlier efforts is that it covers what I consider to be the best stuff in alphabetical order by label and catalogue number. It isn't therefore ranked in order of "superiority" - if it was, you'd all be asking why *Israelites* wasn't top of the list.

Before we kick off, I should just mention why there isn't a similar hit parade for albums. Basically, there are two reasons for this. First, the bulk of reggae albums were put out by Trojan and Pama during the peak reggae years and, with a few exceptions, most of them are all worth having. Second, and this is really the main reason, a high proportion of original reggae and rock steady LPs are now out of the reach of most people's pockets. I for one never really bothered with 45s until about five years ago when the prices of albums really started to skyrocket. As random examples, LPs like Derrick Morgan's *Seven Letters* on Trojan and Amalgamated's *Jackpot Of Hits* compilation could be found quite easily back then for about six or seven quid a throw but now go for upwards of £25 each. Anyway, enough of my excuses, and on with the boss sounds.

Ackee (first series)

Here was a label that seemed to change its colours from issue to issue! The first release, Rupie Martin's All Stars' *Death In The Arena* is a fast organ instrumental in the Lee Perry mode. Well worth picking up, this one. Otherwise, there were two highly recommended Laurel Aitken issues (*Sin Pon You / Every Night* on ACK 106 and *Pussy Got Thirteen Life / Single Man* (ACK 104) on white labels, Dave Barker's Studio One cut of *Johnny Dollar* (ACK 113) and Girlie And Paul's *Decimilization* on ACK 124, which was a Joe Mansano production. The DJ cuts by Dennis Alcapone and Lizzy are good, but the label as a whole tends to be a bit patchy.

- *Death In The Arena / Natural*
Rupie Martin's All Stars
Ackee ACK 101 (1969)
produced by Junior Lincoln (UK)
Some pressings credit Naturality as the artist.

- *Sin Pon You / Everynight*
Laurel Aitken
Ackee ACK 106 (1969)
produced by Laurel Aitken (UK)
Issued as a white label only.

- *Whispering Bells / Whiplash*
Owen Gray / Clancy's All Stars
Ackee ACK 123 (1971)
produced by Clancy Collins (UK)
B side is in fact *Jacket* by Dave Barker.

Amalgamated

This is one of the few labels with hardly a duff release. As Island / B & C's (and later Trojan / B & C's) outlet for JA productions from Joe Gibbs (aka Joel Gibson), the label notched up a total of some 73 releases by the likes of Lee Perry, The Pioneers, Ken Parker and Stranger And Gladdy. Probably the only real blip in the series is on the B side of The Leaders' *Tit For Tat* (AMG 804) which is a gospel thing by The Marvetts. LP wise, there was a Pioneers album, *Greetings From The Pioneers*, and two compilations, *Explosive Rock Steady* and *Jackpot Of Hits*, all of which are well worth having.

- *El Casino Royale / Dee's Special*
Lynn Tait & the Jets (with Count Machuki)
Amalgamated AMG 810 (1968)
produced by Joel Gibson (Joe Gibbs)
A side can also be found on WIRL's *Club Rock Steady* compilation album (ILP 965).

- *Give Me Little Loving / This Is Soul*
The Pioneers / Lynn Tait & the Jets
Amalgamated AMG 811 (1968)
produced by Joe Gibbs
A side also to be found on The Pioneers'
Greetings From . . . LP on Amalgamated
(AMGLP 2003).

- *Now I'm All Alone / Fall And Rise*
Victor Morris
Amalgamated AMG 813 (1968)
produced by Joe Gibbs
A very interesting disc - if you can find it!

- *Long Shot / Dip And Fall Back*
The Pioneers
Amalgamated AMG 814 (1968)
produced by Joe Gibbs
Also on *Club Rock Steady*.

- *Jackpot / Kimble*
The Pioneers / The Creators (actually by Lee Perry)
Amalgamated AMG 821 (August 1968)
produced by Joe Gibbs
A side on *Greetings From The Pioneers* and later re-issued on the label's short-lived CSP series
to promote the *Jackpot Of Hits* compilation (CSP 3), which it was also on!

- *Hurry Come Up / Off Track*
The Crashers
Amalgamated AMG 834 (February 1969)
produced by Joe Gibbs
Amalgamated's first release of '69, The Crashers were none other than The Ethiopians. Also on
Jackpot Of Hits.

- *Them A Laugh And A Ki Ki / The Hippy's Are Here*
The Soul Mates / The Hippy Boys
Amalgamated AMG 836 (March 1969)
produced by Joe Gibbs
The Soul Mates was one of the many pseudonyms for The Pioneers. This track is also on
Tighten Up Volume 2.

- *Wreck A Buddy / Push It In*
The Soul Sisters / The Versatiles
Amalgamated AMG 839 (May 1969)
produced by Joe Gibbs
A side is very similar to the Buster-produced *Pon Pon Song* by The Sexy Girls on Dice (CC 100).
Also on *Tighten Up volume 2*.

- *On The Move / Jump It Up*
The Soul Mates
Amalgamated AMG 842 (June 1969)
produced by Joe Gibbs
As these are largely instrumental tracks, the credits are almost certainly wrong. The flip side is possibly by The Viceroys.

- *Franco Nero / Version*
Joe Gibbs' All Stars (A side is actually by Count Machuki)
Amalgamated AMG 858 (1970)
produced by Joe Gibbs
The same rhythm track was later used for (Sir) Lord Comic's *Jack Of My Trade* on Pressure Beat (PB 5507).

Attack

Attack was originally set up by Graeme Goodall, who also ran the Doctor Bird group of labels. The early issues on Attack from '69 and '70 are rarely seen these days. Don't pass up copies of *Su Su Su* by The Soul Directions on ATT 8011 as the group were actually The Pioneers, or Winston Groov(e)y's *You Can't Turn Your Back On Me* on ATT 8019 as Pama Dice does his thing on the B side with *The Worm*. Otherwise, much of the label was given over to Goodall's Philligree stable, which included Symarip, Family Circle, Ray Martell and Nyah Shuffle. Most were pretty run-of-the-mill. Attack resurfaced again in '72 as a Trojan label with some good DJ releases by Carey And Lloyd and Dennis Alcapone.

- *The Worm / You Can't Turn Your Back On Me*
Pama Dice / Winston Groovey
Attack ATT 8019 (1970)
produced by Laurel Aitken (UK)
This is not the same as Lloyd Robinson's *The Worm* on Camel (CA 41). Groovey's number is mediocre-ish. A lot of early Attack stuff, particularly by the likes of Family Circle and other Philligree stable acts, is pretty lame.

BAF

Dutch group The Cats had a minor UK chart hit with a reggae version of *Swan Lake* in '69 on this short-lived independent. Beware of anything by Ray Pereira and Four Lads And A Lass (!). In fact, if it's not by The Cats it's not worth bothering about.

Opposite page: The Pioneers (photo by Barry Plummer)

Bamboo

The most memorable sounds on this label came early in the series. Some plaintive vocals from Ken Parker with *My Whole World Is Falling Down*, Alton Ellis's *Better Example* and the Heptones' *I Shall Be Released* (actually a re-issue from the Studio One label). Bamboo also housed Laurel Aitken's *Moon Rock*. A lot of good instrumentals by Jackie Mittoo and Sound Dimension, but also the odd roots tune by the likes of Burning Spear (*Door Peeper*) and The Heptones (*Choice Of Colours* and *Message From A Blackman*). A label well worth collecting (as it's 99% Studio One material) but with a lot of slower, funky reggae type efforts.

- *My Whole World Is Falling Down / Choking Kind*
Ken Parker
Bamboo BAM 1 (1969)
produced by Coxsone Dodd
Also on Attack / Bamboo's Big Bamboo sampler (BDLPS 217) put out in '74.

- *Better Example / Lick It Back*
Alton Ellis / Duke Morgan
Bamboo BAM 2 (1969)
produced by Coxsone Dodd
One of Alton's best cuts from his two year sojourn at Studio One. Never put on album unfortunately.

- *Moon Rock / Cut Up Munno*
Laurel Aitken
Bamboo BAM 16 (1970)
produced by Laurel Aitken (UK)
A real Bamboo one-off, this was issued on white label only and is a real rarity.

- *Dancing Groove / Peanut Butter*
Jackie Mittoo / Black And George
Bamboo BAM 51 (1970)
produced by Coxsone Dodd
A side is the late Jackie's organ version of Delroy Wilson's *Dancing Mood* on Island (WI 3013), but the flip is actually better!

BAMBOO BOSS 10

THIS WEEK	LAST WEEK			
(1)	(1)	Dark Of The Moon.	Jackie Mittoo.	Bam. 17.
(2)	(2)	No More.	Omen.	Ack. 102.
(3)	(3)	My Whole World Is Falling Down.	Ken Parker.	Bam. 1,
(4)	(4)	Poison Ivy.	Sound Dimension.	Bam. 18.
(5)	(5)	How Can I Trust You.	Cables.	Bam. 19.
(6)	(10)	Love At First Sight.	Brentford Road All Stars.	Bam. 23.
(7)	(9)	Give Peace A Chance.	Freedom Singers.	Bam. 21.
(8)	(6)	Doctor Sappa Too.	Sound Dimension.	Bam. 11.
(9)	(7)	I Shall Be Released.	Heptones.	Bam. 11.
(10)	(8)	Baby Face.	Sound Dimension.	Bam. 7.

FAST MOVERS

Some Day We'll Be Together/ Everyday People.	Joy Roberts. Sound Dimension.	Bam. 30.
Soul Shake.	Brentford Road All Stars.	Bam. 25.
Love Me Tonight.	The Soulites.	Bam. 27.
Walkie Talkie/Moan And Groan	The Ethiopians.	Bam. 26.

NEW RELEASES

Gold Dust.	Jackie Mittoo.	Bam. 20.
Girl Of My Dream.	Larry & Alvin.	Bam. 22.
Can I Change My Mind (Inst.)	Brentford Road All Stars.	Bam. 31.
Good Ways.	Three Tones.	Bam. 32.
Use What I've Got.	Red River Band.	Bam 35.

BAMBOO RECORDS LTD
88 STROUD GREEN ROAD
FINSBURY PARK LONDON · N.4   01-263 0411

- **Rhythm Rebellion / Reggae Children**
Lord Comic / Roy Richards
Bamboo BAM 66 (1970)
produced by Coxsone Dodd
The only DJ track on the label (most were off-loaded onto the sister label, Banana).

Banana
The releases on Banana were of a similar nature to those on Bamboo, except that there was a more liberal sprinkling of Studio One DJ sides by the likes of Dennis Alcapone, King Stitt and King Sporty, all of which are worth picking up. Highlights include The Classics' *Mr Fire Coal Man* (actually by The Wailing Souls) and Alton Ellis' *Sunday Coming*, but as with Bamboo, if slower reggae isn't your bag then most of the label's output probably won't appeal to you.

- **Mr. Fire Coal Man / Version**
The Wailing Souls (miscredited to The Classics) / Sound Dimension
Bamboo BA 331 (1971)
produced by Coxsone Dodd
This one really eats its way into the brain.

- **Picture On The Wall / Version**
Freddy McKay / Sound Dimension
Bamboo BA 348 (1971)
produced by Coxsone Dodd
One of the best from the late great Freddy. Lee Perry also cut a version of it using the vocal talents of the great Carl (Rass) Dawkins on Upsetter (US 368)

Big
A Trojan / B & C label specialising in Rupie Edwards productions. The label initially veered towards the more commercial end of reggae with its Gaylads and Dabby Dobson outings. The most favourable record on the label is *Music Alone Shall Live* by Rupie Edwards' All Stars and the DJ version of it by Keith Cole.

Big Shot
Although this label is generally remembered for The Kingstonians' *Sufferer*, Rudy Mills' *John Jones* and the series of Judge Dread "Big" sides, there were other goodies as well. The Tennors kicked off the label with *Reggae Girl*, and later put out other fast reggae sides such as *Another Scorcher*. Other JA productions

54

worthy of note are The Crystalites' *Biafra* and Derrick Morgan's *Shower Of Rain*. On the UK side of things came The Prophets with *Revenge Of Eastwood*, Patrick And Lloyd's *Return Of The Pollock* and The Saints' *Windy*, making this a very collectable label. There were also three very scarce compilations issued, *Reggae Girl*, *Live It Up* and *Once More*, and an all Lynn Tait And The Jets LP entitled *Glad Sounds*. Definitely one to look out for, but the albums nowadays command price tags of up to £60 each.

● **Reggae Girl / Donkey Trot**
The Tennors / Clive's All Stars
Big Shot BI 501 (December 1968)
produced by A G Murphy (George
     Murphy)
The first release on this classic label.

● **Sufferer / Kiss A Finger**
The Kingstonians
Big Shot BI 508 (January 1969)
produced by Derrick Harriott
Also on *Tighten Up Volume 2*, *Sufferer* was
played at a youth club disco featured in the BBC
Man Alive programme on skinheads from 1969.
Also the title track of a Kingstonians album on
Trojan (TBL 113).

● **John Jones / A Place Called Happiness**
Rudy Mills
Big Shot BI 509 (January 1969)
produced by Derrick Harriott
Also on *Tighten Up Volume 2* and the man's own unbelievably rare *Reggae Hits* LP on Pama (SECO 12). Strangely, Mills seemed to have completely disappeared from the reggae scene after the Sixties came to a close.

● **Biafra / Drop Pon**
The Crystalites
Big Shot BI 510 (February 1969)
produced by Derrick Harriott
A rousing organ instrumental also to be found on Harriott's Trojan compilation LP *The Undertaker* (TBL 114). His Big Shot productions were soon to be given over to the fledgling Song Bird label.

● **Windy / Part 2**
The Saints
Big Shot BI 522 (1969)
produced by Les Foster (UK)
A reggae version of *Tom Hark*, this probably provided the inspiration for The Piranhas' version released during the Two Tone era.

Reggae Top 25

1 HOLLY HOLY
   (1) Fabulous Flames (Clan Disc)
2 RIVERS OF BABYLON
   (2) Melodians (Summit)
3 DOPPY CONQUER
   (3) Bob Marley & The Wailers (Duke Reid)
4 SAY ME SAY
   (14) Justine Hines (Duke Reid)
5 WEAR YOU TO THE BALL
   (7) Hugh Roy & John Holt (Duke Reid)
6 FEEL ALRIGHT
   (6) The Cables (Harry J.)
7 GROOVY SITUATION
   (5) Derrick Harriet (Song Bird)
8 I CAN DO IT TOO
   (11) The Twinkle Brothers (Jackpot)
9 PEOPLES CHOICE
   (10) Winston Williams (Jackpot)
10 THERE'S SOMETHING ABOUT YOU
   (9) Lloyd Charmers (Trojan)
11 GET TOGETHER
   (8) Carl Dorkins (Duke Reid)
12 D.J. CHOICE
   (12) Winston Williams (Jackpot)
13 I NEED YOUR SWEET INSPIRATION
   (14) Pioneers (Trojan)
14 MOVEMENTS
   (13) Jo Gibbs (Amalgamated)
15 SAME THING ALL OVER
   (17) The Untouchables (Upsetter)
16 TAKE A LETTER TO MARIA
   (21) Dandy (Trojan)
17 WHAT GREATER LOVE
   (15) Teddy Brown (Trojan)
18 BITTERNESS OF LIFE
   (—) Bruce Ruffin (Summit)
19 HONEY HUSH
   (22) Millie (Trojan)
20 TOP SECRET
   (—) Winston Wright (Technique)
21 BAND OF GOLD
   (16) Marcia Griffiths (Harry J.)
22 MONTEGO BAY
   (19) Freddie Notes & The Rudies (Trojan)
23 MO'BAY
   (25) Selwyn Baptiste (Black Swan)
24 NO BAPTISM
   (20) Ethopians (Song Bird)
25 MUSIC KEEP ON PLAYING
   (23) G.G. Allstars (G.G.)

- *Queen Of The World / Top Of The World (Version)*
Lloyd And Claudette / The Prophets
Big Shot BI 546 (1970)
produced by Bryan & Shrowder (UK)
The A side was based largely on Lloyd Robinson's *The Worm*. Also issued on Trojan's *Tighten Up Volume 3* (TBL 145) and *Queen Of The World* compilations (TBL 136).

- *Return Of The Pollock / Concorde*
Patrick And Lloyd/The Prophets
Big Shot BI 550 (1970)
produced by Bryan & Shrowder (UK)
A real good slice of skinhead reggae. Both sides are also on Trojan's *Queen Of The World* LP.

- *Out The Light Baby / Mosquito One*
Dennis Alcapone
Big Shot BI 572 (1971)
produced by Byron Smith
Produced by Duke Reid's associate Byron Smith, *Mosquito One* is a toast over Nora Dean's *Barbwire* and is rather better than the A side, which is a cut to Joya Landis' *Out The Light* on Trojan. *Mosquito One* was also available on Punch (PH 36) but this pressing is much harder to find.

Blue Beat

Blue Beat's glory days of ska were more or less over by the dawn of '67, but Prince Buster's rock steady outings kept the label alive for a while longer - his *Judge Dread*, *Too Hot* and *Ghost Dance* were classics of their kind. Melodisc obviously felt that the term "Blue Beat" was rather outdated and replaced the label with Fab. Even so, Buster's *Al Capone* was a big UK ska hit for him on Blue Beat that year, having originally appeared in '65.

- *Judge Dread / Waiting For My Rude Girl*
Prince Buster / Fitzroy Campbell
Blue Beat BB 387 (1967)
produced by Prince Buster
Triggering off a series of discs on the same theme, this is still so popular that a British television commercial has adapted and bastardised it. Also on the Prince's *Judge Dread* LP (BBLP 809) and *Fabulous Greatest Hits* on Fab (MS1). B side was actually titled *Sitting In A Ya-Ya* and was based around an early Lee Dorsey number.

- *Soul Serenade / Too Hot*
Prince Buster & The All Stars
Blue Beat BB 390 (1967)
produced by Prince Buster
The B side is definitely the better of the two. Also on *Fabulous Greatest Hits* and later covered by
The Specials.

Blue Cat

Blue Cat was one of those mixed bag labels consisting mainly of productions by Coxsone Dodd, Joe Gibbs, Bunny Lee and Harry J, and these days they're as rare as hens' teeth. Most that I've heard are very good. Ones to avoid are Lance Hannibal's dire *Read The News* (which Trojan re-issued on at least three occasions!), and The Righteous Twins' gospel track, *If I Could Hear My Mother.*

- *I've Got Your Number / Hot Shot*
Dermott Lynch
Blue Cat BS 101 (1968)
produced by Charles Ross
Great rock steady number also to be found on
WIRL's *Club Rock Steady* compilation.

- *Girls Like Dirt / She Is Leaving*
Slim Smith & The Uniques / Glen Adams
Blue Cat BS 126 (August 1968)
produced by Bunny Lee
One of Slim's best, notable for its relatively long bridge. The B side is in fact believed to be by
Alva Lewis, later of The Upsetters.

- *Nana / I May Never See My Baby*
The Slickers / Martin Riley
Blue Cat BS 134 (1968)
produced by Eric Barnet / Bunny Lee
With George Agard on vocals, this was one of Blue Cat's biggest sellers and went some way
towards crossing over to the white market in the UK. Also on volume one of Trojan's *The Trojan Story* triple album (TALL 100).

- *Loving Reggae / Musical Beat*
The Maytones / Roy Samuel
Blue Cat BS 152 (February 1969)
produced by Alvin Ranglin
A fast one from The Maytones, which typified their driving vocals during the reggae era. Nicely
tucked away on Trojan's *Reggae Flight 404* compilation of Ranglin-produced material (TBL 115).

- *Dig It Up / This Life Make Me (Wonder)*
The Sparkers / Delroy Wilson
Blue Cat BS 155 (April 1969)
produced by George Regent
This was the vocal to Ranfold Williams' *Code It* on BS 154B (the flip to The Slickers' *Frying Pan*).
Nice B side too.

- *2,000 Tons Of T.N.T / Botheration*
The GG Rhythm Section / The Maytones
Blue Cat BS 165 (June 1969)
produced by Vernon Buckley / Alvin Ranglin
Largely a flute instrumental with vocal interjections, this was actually by Vernon Buckley, lead
singer of The Maytones. On the flip, yet another song called *Botheration*.

Bread

A rather non-descript Trojan / B & C subsidiary, this label issued a few titles by
Del Davis, Count Prince Miller, and Jackie Edwards, but is not particularly
collectable. The most favourable record on the label that I've heard is Edwards'
cover of Billy Stewart's soul standard, *I Do Love You* from '72, but it's certainly not
skinhead reggae.

Bullet

Another mixed bag label as far as
producers and artists (both JA and UK)
are concerned. Nicky Thomas had his
first discs released on Bullet, a year or
so before *Love Of The Common People*,
and his *Run Mr Nigel* is quite good.
Otherwise, the issues by The Ebony
Sisters (particularly *Let Me Tell You
Boy*), Dennis Walks (*Heart Don't Leap*)
Lloyd Charmers, and The Hippy Boys
are worth collecting. Pama issued a
compilation of a dozen Bullet cuts
entitled *World Of Bullet* and, if you can
ever find it, it provides an excellent
opportunity to acquire the best output of
a sometimes patchy label.

- *Let Me Tell You Boy / Mannix*
Ebony Sisters / Rhythm Rulers
Bullet BU 401 (1969)
produced by Harry Mudie
One of the very few female groups of the time, The Ebonies could usually be relied on to come up
with a good tune. Also on Moodisc's *Mudie's Mood* compilation of Harry Mudie productions (TBL
132) and Pama's *World Of Bullet* (SECO 19). I Roy later DJ'd it for Moodisc (Mu 3512).

- *Heart Don't Leap / I Am Sorry*
Dennis Walks / The Clarendonians
Bullet BU 402 (1969)
produced by Harry Mudie
Also on *Mudie's Mood* and *World Of Bullet* and subject to a later I Roy cover. The B side is a rock steady cut.

- *V-Rocket / Smile*
The Fabions
Bullet BU 410 (1969)
produced by George Murphy
The one and only outing in the UK for The Fabions was this version of The Tennors' *Another Scorcher* which appeared on Big Shot (BI 517).

Caltone

A subsidiary of R & B Discs, Honey Boy Martin's *Dreader Than Dread* (also on volume one of *The Trojan Story*) and Roy Shirley's *Get On The Ball* are, to my mind, the two most crucial cuts on this label of just 22 issues. Caltone dealt mainly with the work of JA producer Ken Lock (spelt "Calnek" on the labels for some strange reason), and also housed a very early Bunny Lee production in the form of The Heptones' *School Girls*. Also worthy of note is Lloyd And The Groovers' *Meet Me On The Corner,* which Dennis Brown reggae-fied in '72 for the Randy's label. Avoid The Pioneers' *I Love No Other Girl* because it's a soul track, but otherwise Caltone is a good bet if you're into rock steady.

- *Sounds And Soul / Get On The Ball*
Johnny Moore With Tommy McCook And The Supersonics / Roy Shirley With The Caltone Studio Orchestra
Caltone TONE 101 (1967)
produced by Ken Lock (aka Lack)
Amazingly relegated to the B side, *Get On The Ball* knocks the fairly run-of-the-mill horns instrumental on the top side for six. Shirley was seen performing this live on the *Aquarius* programme on British reggae made in '76.

- *In The Mood / Dreader Than Dread*
Dandy And His Group / Honeyboy Martin And The Voices With Tommy McCook And The Supersonics
Caltone TONE 1103 (1967)
produced by Ken Lock / Dandy (UK)
Dandy's pedestrian version of Glen Miller's standard was the top side but *Dreader Than Dread* is really the classic here and was featured on volume one of *The Trojan Story*. Utilising the rhythm from The Tartans' *It's All Right* (TONE 117), it was one of the best discs issued on the rude boy theme.

59

Camel

Another Pama tour de force, Camel's first disc was The Techniques' superb *Who You Gonna Run To* (with Bruce Ruffin on lead vocals). There were several excellent Lee Perry productions (identified by the word "Scratch" at the bottom of the label), a few by Lloyd Daley including Jackie Mittoo's *Dark (Side) Of The Sun*, a Derrick Harriott produced *In This World* by The Federals, and a couple of Alvin Ranglin's (particularly good is *Feel It* by The Ebony Sisters, which they also did on GG under the name Paulette And Gee). In fact, apart from a few of the '70-'71 Owen Gray sides, which are mediocre, Camel was one of Pama's finest. Stranger Cole's *Crying Every Night* from '71 is also worth having as it's a vocal cut using U Roy's *Tom Drunk* rhythm to be found on the Duke Reid label. Again, Pama issued a compilation LP of Camel tracks entitled *An Oasis of Sounds: The Best of Camel*, which is now unbelievably rare.

- ### *Who You Gonna Run To / Hi-There*
The Techniques / Riley's All Stars
Camel CA 10 (1969)
produced by Winson Riley
Bruce Ruffin handled the vocal honours on this one which, despite its number, was the first one on the label. Great song too. Also found on a number of Pama albums, namely *A Gift From Pama* (SECO 20), *The Best Of Camel* (SECO 18), volume two of *Reggae Hits '69* (ECO 11) and *Sixteen Dynamic Reggae Hits* (PMP 2015). The Palmer Brothers certainly got their money's worth on this one!

- ### *Down In The Park / Love Oh Love*
The Inspirations
Camel CA 11 (1969)
produced by Lee Perry
Nice vocals on classic Upsetters' rhythms. Also on volume two of *Reggae Hits '69*.

- ### *Taste Of Killing / My Mob*
The Upsetters
Camel CA 13 (1969)
produced by Lee Perry
Some of these early Camel releases are so good they're almost double A sides. You can find both these scorching organ instrumentals on Pama's *Clint Eastwood* LP (PSP 1014).

- ### *Strange Whispering / Hard To Handle*
The West Indians / Carl Dawkins
Camel CA 16 (1969)
produced by Lee Perry
Eric Donaldson of *Cherry Oh Baby* fame was lead vocalist with this lot for a time. A very fast reggae number, also on *Best Of Camel*.

Opposite page: Stranger Cole, Kingston Waterfront, 1992 (photo by Maverick)

- *History / Just Be Alone*
Harry And Radcliffe
Camel CA 26 (1969)
producer unknown
A great reggae cover of Sam Cooke's *Wonderful World*, this also reputedly came out on a Punch 45 (PH 8). Also on *A Gift From Pama*, this was the duo's only UK release and its origins are somewhat shrouded in mystery.

- *Sentimental Reason / Lover Girl*
The Maytones
Camel CA 27 (1969)
produced by A Ranglin
Superb stuff from a musical force to be reckoned with. Also on volume one of Pama's *This Is Reggae* (PSP 1003) and Trojan's *Reggae Flight 404* LPs. But has anyone ever seen one on Explosion (supposedly EX 2013)?

- *Cat Nip / Cooyah*
The Hippy Boys
Camel CA 29 (1969)
produced by Lloyd Charmers (aka Lloyd Tyrell)
This guy was producing some excellent skinhead reggae during '69-'71 and this frantic organ instrumental was no exception. Also on volume one of Pama's *This Is Reggae*, while the flip was on the company's mega-rare *House In Session* album of Charmers' productions (SECO 25).

- *Beware Of Bad Dogs / Short Cut*
The Soul Mates
Camel CA 33 (1969)
produced by Glen Adams
These sides were both in fact by Glen himself and were similar to the stuff he was knocking out with The Upsetters.

- *Crying / It Must Come*
Stranger Cole / Dennis Alcapone And Delroy Wilson
Camel CA 72 (1971)
produced by Byron Smith / Bunny Lee
One of Stranger's best reggae cuts, this rhythm was also used for U Roy And Hopeton Lewis' *Tom Drunk* on Duke Reid (DR 2517). Trojan / B & C also put it out on their short-lived Spinning Wheel subsidiary (SW 109). The flip is Alcapone's DJ outing over the late Delroy Wilson's classic *Better Must Come* on Jackpot (JP 763).

Clandisc

This was Trojan / B & C's exclusive outlet for Clancy Eccles productions and is probably best remembered for its three compilation LPs, *Fire Corner*, *Herbsman Reggae* and *Foolish Fool*, as well as Clancy's own *Freedom*. Its King Stitt output (*Herbsman Shuffle*, *Vigorton Two* and the Western-flavoured *The Ugly One*) is essential skinhead reggae fare, as are Clancy's own early tracks with house band The Dynamites. His later discs like *Africa* and *Rod Of Correction*, from '70 and '71 respectively, espoused the Rasta philosophy and are not quite as collectable.

- **Mr Midnight (Skokiaan) / Who Yeah**
The Dynamites / King Stitt
Clandisc CLA 200 (1969)
produced by Clancy Eccles
A slow and moody organ version of an age-old Latin-American tune, this is also to be found on Trojan's *Fire Corner* LP of Eccles' material on Clandisc (TTL 21).

- **The World Needs Loving / Dollar Train**
Clancy Eccles
Clandisc CLA 201 (1969)
produced by Clancy Eccles
Two scorching sides here, both of which are on his *Freedom* LP on Clandisc (TTL 22). Do yourself a favour and get the album as well.

- **Vigorton 2 / Mount Zion**
King Stitt / The Dynamites
Clandisc CLA 203 (1969)
produced by Clancy Eccles
This was Stitt's follow-up to *Fire Corner* and was also on the *Fire Corner* album as well as (much later) *20 Tighten Ups* (TRLS 90).

- **Foolish Fool / On The Street**
Cynthia Richards / King Stitt
Clandisc CLA 204 (1969)
produced by Clancy Eccles
Female singers have long been under-represented in Jamaican music, but Cynthia Richards was certainly among the few frontrunners in the field. Also on Trojan's *Foolish Fool* LP (TBL 123), which was yet another of the company's Eccles compilations bearing the Clandisc label.

- **The Ugly One (aka Van Cleef) / Beat Dance**
King Stitt / King Stitt And Clancy Eccles
Clandisc CLA 206 (1969)
produced by Clancy Eccles
From a time when the spoken introductions were almost as popular as the records themselves, this was another Spaghetti Western styled 45. Also on Trojan's final Clandisc compilation LP of Eccles' material, *Herbsman Reggae* (TBL 124). The flip was actually called *Dance Beat*.

- **Herbsman Shuffle / Don't Mind Me**
King Stitt And Andy Capp / Higgs And Wilson
Clandisc CLA 207 (1970)
produced by Clancy Eccles
Two manic DJs tell us about "the weed" - one of the earliest discs to do so. Trojan made maximum mileage out of this classic - it's on *Tighten Up Volume 3*, *Fire Corner* and *Herbsman Reggae*. Veteran duo Higgs And Wilson have a nice tune on the flip.

Collins Down Beat

This short run of just a dozen or so releases is not to be sneezed at as it just brims over with marvellous rock steady with some superb sides from Owen Gray, Lester Sterling and The Uniques (albeit without the late great Slim Smith). The Uniques' *I'm A Fool For You* was a Bunny Lee production, as was Glen Adams' *Cool Cool Rock Steady* (although it was in fact by Don Tony Lee!). Highly recommended for rock steady fans.

- *Dry The Water From Your Eyes / I'm A Fool For You*
Clancy Collins / The Uniques
Collins Down Beat CR 002 (1967)
produced by Clancy Collins / Bunny Lee
A nice slice of UK rock steady, with an early Uniques number minus Slim Smith on the flip.

- *I'm So Lonely / Shock Steady*
Owen Gray And Sir Collins And His Band / Reco, Sir Collins And J Satch
Collins Down Beat CR 004 (1967)
produced by Clancy Collins
Owen Gray's soulful vocals were particularly well suited to rock steady and this was one of his best cuts in that style.

- *Cool Cool Rock Steady / Girl I Will Be Leaving*
Glen Adams / Owen Gray
Collins Down Beat CR 006 (1968)
produced by Bunny Lee / Clancy Collins
Actually by early DJ, Don Tony Lee, although Adams might be on it somewhere! More soulful sounds from Owen Gray on the flip.

Columbia Blue Beat

Apart from the penultimate issue on the label, this EMI offshoot put out UK productions (mainly by Siggy Jackson) by The Mopeds (*Whisky And Soda*), Blue Rivers And The Maroons, Laurel Aitken and The Bees (which I think was yet another psuedonym for The Pyramids). Most of them sound like Geno Washington trying to do ska and have a very brassy feel. A bit too commercial for my tastes, but very popular with collectors at the moment. I don't think they sold particularly well as the ones I've come across have usually been demonstration or promotional discs, indicating that released copies probably only sold a few hundred each. For my money, the best release was the penultimate one, The Bleechers' *Adam and Eve* which was a Leslie Kong production. The only LP on the label was by Blue Rivers And The Maroons.

Coxsone

This was initially one of Island / B & C's two exclusive outlets for Coxsone Dodd's Studio One productions (its sister label, Studio One, is covered later). Apart from a couple of slow soul outings by Tony Gregory, there's hardly a duff issue from around a hundred releases. Anyone already collecting Coxsone releases will know that the same three or four issues seem to turn up every time - The Soul Agents' *Get Ready, It's Rock Steady*, Jackie Mittoo's *Ram Jam*, Cool Spoon's *Yakety Yak*, and The Tennors' *Pressure And Slide* are the most common. These are all highly recommended, but other issues by the likes of Sound Dimension, The Heptones, Ken Boothe, Alton Ellis and The Gaylads rarely ever turn up. In fact, if you seriously want to collect Coxsone label output, you'll need a big bank balance.

Some of the albums go for a fortune these days, and expect to pay around £30 each for the *Blue Beat Special* and *Reggae Special* compilation LPs, which are by far the most common. The latter is the best bet as it contains some of the best skinhead reggae cuts from the final stages of the label (when it was run by Trojan / B & C) like Marcia Griffiths' *Feel Like Jumping*, The Sound Dimension's *Scorcia* and *More Scorcia*, and Roy And Enid's *Reggae For Days* and *Rocking Time*. Beware of JA repressings of Coxsone and Studio One albums as they're often completely remixed with a more modern feel and the quality generally leaves a lot to be desired.

• *Get Ready, It's Rock Steady / Smile Like An Angel*
The Soul Agents / Bop And The Beltones
Coxsone CS 7007 (1967)
produced by Coxsone Dodd
One of the most common 45s on Coxsone, this can also be found on the Coxsone compilation of the same name (CSL 8007).

• *The Rock / Harder On The Rock*
Jeff Dixon / The Hamboys
Coxsone CS 7015 (1967)
produced by Coxsone Dodd
An early DJ-styled effort from the late Jeff Dixon. Also on the Coxsone compilation *Reggae Special* (CSP 2) from '69.

• *Pressure And Slide / One Stop*
The Jennors (The Tennors) / The Soul Brothers
Coxsone CS 7024 (1967)
produced by Coxsone Dodd
A sterling piece of rock steady which used the rhythm to Prince Buster's *Shaking Up Orange Street* (aka *Sweet Pea*) on Fab. *Pressure And Slide* was later included on the *Reggae Special* LP and Melodisc's rare *12 Carat Gold* compilation (MLP 12-217).

- *River Jordan / Swing Easy*
The Basies / The Soul Vendors
Coxsone CS 7034 (1967)
produced by Coxsone Dodd
The B side is a stepping horns instrumental with an Eastern flavour, and is the pick of the two. It was included on one of Island's few decent compilations of vintage material, *The Rock Steady Years, '66-'68*, in 1980 and now deleted. The Soul Vendors were formerly The Soul Brothers.

- *Feel Like Jumping / Thundering Vibrations*
Marcia Griffiths / Horace Taylor
Coxsone CS 7055 (July 1968)
produced by Coxsone Dodd
This one will definitely put you in a jumping mood. Also on *Reggae Special*, another Coxsone compilation entitled *Ride Me Donkey* (CSL 8015) as well as *Club Rock Steady*.

- *Scorcha / Hold Me Baby*
Sound Dimension / Basil Daley
Coxsone CS 7083 (1969)
produced by Coxsone Dodd
This used Larry And Alvin's *Nanny Goat* rhythm and featured DJ Carey Johnson, although it wasn't a full-blown DJ track. Also on *Reggae Special*.

- *Reggae For Days / Holy Moses*
Roy And Enid
Coxsone CS 7088 (April 1969)
produced by Coxsone Dodd
Enid was actually Enid Cumberland of Keith And Enid fame who were the Nina And Frederick of early JA music (if you remember Nina And Frederick that is). Also on *Reggae Special*.

- *Mother Aitken / What A Love*
Dodd's All Stars
Coxsone CS 7096 (June 1969)
produced by Coxsone Dodd
Mother Aitken was a frantic fast reggae vocal by Lord Power and is really too good to be overlooked. Denzil Laing (more usually a percussionist) does the vocal honours on the flip.

Crab

Another Pama subsidiary, Crab put out around 65 45s between '68 and '71. Derrick Morgan was featured heavily with some 18 releases including the great *Moon Hop*, *Make It Tan Deh* and *River To The Bank*, and The Versatiles' *Children Get Ready* (the first on the label) and *Spread Your Bed* are also worthy of mention. Towards the end of the series the label started issuing UK recordings by Winston Groov(e)y, D D Dennis (aka Denzil Dennis) and U B Barrett and some of these are worth a miss. I recently came across a Trinidadian copy of one of Winston Groov(e)y's Crab discs so Pama's net obviously spread further than these fair shores! A compilation LP of Crab cuts entitled *Crab's Biggest Hits* included tracks by The Ethiopians, Ernest Wilson, The Viceroys and Val Bennett and gathers together the best of the label's '69 output.

- *Children Get Ready / Someone To Love*

The Versatiles

Crab CR 1 (1968)

produced by Bunny Barrett

Great record which found its way onto volume one of *Reggae Hits '69* (ECO 3) and *Crab Biggest Hits* (ECO 2). The flip also came out on Island (WI 3142).

Above: Derrick Morgan, one of skinhead reggae's biggest stars.

- *River To The Bank / Reggae Limbo*

Derrick Morgan / Peter King

Crab CR 3 (1968)

produced by Derrick Morgan

Reggae-fied version of a traditional JA folk song which Baba Brooks ska'd earlier as *Bank To Bank*. Also on volume one of *Reggae Hits '69*, *Crab Biggest Hits* and his own *Derrick Morgan In London* LP (ECO 10), all on Pama's excellent Economy series.

- **Reggae Hit The Town / Ding Dong Bell**
The Ethiopians
Crab CR 4 (1968)
produced by Harry Robinson
A solid gold classic, this one. Robinson was a British former rock 'n' roll bandleader who later found his way into West Indian music and did the arrangements on some of the early Millie Small records on Fontana. Personally, I doubt whether he actually produced such authentic sounds as this, but I'm ready to stand corrected if anyone out there knows different. Also on *Crab Biggest Hits*, volume one of *Reggae Hits '69* and another Pama compilation entitled *The Lovely Dozen* (PSP 1001).

- **Run Girl Run / The Drifter**
G G (George) Grossett / Dennis Walks
Crab CR 10 (1969)
produced by Harry Mudie
Both sides are well worth having here. Mudie was still cutting versions of *Drifter* in the mid-Seventies (*Car Pound Drifter*, *Midnight Drifter*, etc). *Run Girl Run* can be found on *Crab Biggest Hits* and volume two of *Reggae Hits '69*.

CRAB

Beverley Music
(P) 1969
45 RPM
CRAB 28 (1)
HARD TIME
D. Morgan
DERRICK MORGAN
Pama Records Productions

- **When There Is You / My Woman's Love**
The Melodians / Slim Smith & The Uniques
Crab CR 15 (1969)
produced by Winston Lowe
Tucked away on the flip of a very average Melodians' track, *My Woman's Love* was quite an elaborate without strings production with Slim's powerful vocals very much to the fore.

- **Hold Down / Who Will She Be?**
The Kingstonians / Barry York
Crab CR 19 (1969)
produced by Derrick Harriott
Very hard, very ethnic and very bassy - typical of The Kingstonians' brand of music. Trojan also put this out on their *Sufferer* LP of Kingstonians' cuts (TBL 113), while Pama put it out on *A Gift From Pama* and *Sixteen Dynamic Reggae Hits* (PMP 2015).

- **Brother Ram Goat / What A Condition**
Theo Beckford / The Starlighters
Crab CR 25 (1969)
produced by Theo Beckford
Not a well-known one, but well worth tracking down. Basically fast reggae over a nicely repetitive vocal, complete with made-in-the-studio goat imitations!

- ***Moon Hop / Harris Wheel***
Derrick Morgan / The Reggaeites
Crab CR 32 (1969)
produced by Derrick Morgan
Crab's biggest seller and a tiny UK chart hit. Symarip plagiarised it for their *Skinhead Moonstomp* on Treasure Isle. Sadly, if it wasn't for this one (good though it was), *Moon Hop* could've been a Top 20 hit. You can actually hear a bell ringing at the end of this (and other Pama tracks), probably signifying the "cut-off" point! Also on volume one of *This Is Reggae* and Derrick's *Moon Hop* set (PSP 1006).

- ***A Night At The Hop / Telephone***
Derrick Morgan
Crab CR 44 (1970)
produced by Derrick Morgan (UK)
This was just about Derrick's last great track in skinhead reggae terms. Taken from his sorely disappointing *Moon Hop* LP (sorry Del old son), it's a bit of a shouter with a much more British-sounding backing track, suggesting perhaps that the rhythms for his earlier Pama material were actually laid in JA rather than over here.

Creole
This label was initially distributed by Trojan / B & C, but eventually became a successful independent pop outlet in the mid to late Seventies, garnering several UK Top 40 hits. There were just six releases between '70 and '71, the first of which by Lloyd Seivright was gospel. There were a few by The Pyramids, one by Nat Cole, and one which was reputedly an early Augustus Pablo outing when he played keyboards instead of melodica.

Crystal
A short-lived President off-shoot, only *Sherman* by The Cats (see also BAF label) is particularly well known in skinhead circles. There were a couple of others by Horatio Soul and Junior Smith and an LP by a group called The Pavement. Largely an unknown quantity unfortunately.

Direct
A Doctor Bird subsidiary with only four releases to its name, two of which (by The Merrymen) were hi-life calypso, and another was a soul / R & B number by Errol Dixon. Not worth bothering about.

Doctor Bird
This powerhouse of a label covered ska, rock steady and reggae over a run of almost 200 issues. A good selection of productions from Sonia Pottinger, Coxsone Dodd and Duke Reid with almost every artist of note appearing on the label - Alton Ellis, The Wailers, Delroy Wilson, The Silvertones, The Gaylads, The Melodians, Laurel Aitken, Clancy Eccles to name but a few. Be careful of the odd rogue cut like Patsy's *Little Flea*, The Blues Busters' *I've Been Trying*, and Tony Gregory's *Let Me Come On Home* which are not ska, rock steady or reggae.

Be warned also about the quality of some of the earlier pressings, which can often sound really rough on the high notes. For example, I've owned about three mint condition copies of The Silvertones' *True Confession* which all sounded lousy so it's certainly not down to wear and tear. Otherwise, almost everything issued between '67 and '68 is a gem.

The Laurel Aitken 45s such as *Reggae Prayer* and *Heile Heile (The Lion)* are essential skinhead listening, as is his *Fire* LP. One bone of contention I should perhaps mention is that Doctor Bird used a JJ label (intended for JJ Johnson productions, mainly by The Ethiopians) for some of their straight Doctor Bird label issues. Hence, Laurel's *Rise And Fall* appeared on a JJ label, but wasn't a JJ Johnson production. This also happened with releases by The Tennors and The Pyramids and I can only presume that the company had a wagon load of JJ paper labels printed up and felt compelled to use them wherever possible! I've also mentioned this in the JJ and Pyramid label outlines later on.

- *Girl I've Got A Date / The Yellow Basket*
Alton Ellis And The Flames / Tommy McCook & Lynn Tait
Doctor Bird DB 1059 (1967)
produced by Duke Reid
Just one in a string of classics from Alton Ellis produced by "The Trojan" himself for his Treasure Isle label.

- *Stop Them / Deep Down*
Hazel And The Jolly Boys
Doctor Bird DB 1063 (1967)
produced by Sonia Pottinger for Gayfeet Records
A big seller, this isn't quite as good as The Freedom Singers' version of it produced by Coxsone, which only featured on a Studio One compilation over in the UK.

- *Hold Them / Be Good*
Roy Shirley And Lynn Tait's Band
Doctor Bird DB 1068 (1967)
produced by Joe Gibbs
Reputedly his first production and said by some
to be the first ever rock steady record, Gibbs
later re-cut this for release on Amalgamated's *Explosive Rock Steady* album. Prince Buster also tried his hand at it and Ken Boothe cut it as *Feel Good* for Studio One (SO 2000).

- *The Whip / Cool It Amigo*
The Ethiopians
Doctor Bird DB 1096 (1967)
produced by Sonia Pottinger for Gayfeet Records
Along with Roland Alphonso's *Phoenix City*, this was Doctor Bird's other really big seller. Largely an instrumental, it recieved a lot of airplay at fairgrounds around the UK as an accompaniment to a ride called The Whip. Also on volume one of *The Trojan Story* box set.

- *The Lecture / Cantelope Rock*
Jo Jo Bennett And The Fugitives
Doctor Bird DB 1097 (1967)
produced by W.I.R.L (West Indies
Records Ltd)
Another early DJ venture with a very
infectious bass line. Actually a cornet
player, Jo Jo later cut some tremendous
material for Harry Mudie in a completely
instrumental style, including the brilliant
Leaving Rome (TR -7774) .

- *The Train Is Coming Back / So
Fine*
The Gladiators
Doctor Bird DB 1114 (1968)
produced by W.I.R.L
Reputedly their first ever record and
certainly their UK debut. A fine piece of
jumpy rock steady also on *Club Rock
Steady '68.*

- *Put Down Your Fire / Girls Like
Dirt*
The Kingstonians
Doctor Bird DB 1120 (1968)
produced by JJ Johnson
Raw rock steady with some fine vocals.

- *People Funny Boy / Blowing In
The Wind*
Lee Perry / Bert Walters
Doctor Bird DB 1146 (1968)
produced by Lee Perry

WHERE TO HEAR IT . . .

WITH the current boom in bluebeat, the chances are that wherever you live, wherever you go, reggae is the name of the game at your local club.

But true authenticity, the best atmosphere, and certainly the most enjoyable time must be had at house parties.

Next best thing after the house parties are the West Indian clubs. These are to be found in London (especially areas like Brixton, Dalston, Islington, Shepherd's Bush and Lewisham), Birmingham, Manchester, Nottingham, Liverpool and Glasgow, among other cities.

After that come the clubs and ballrooms frequented by that "new-wave mod," the "skinhead." There's one in every town, and all you need do is wait on a main corner and follow the boots, braces and crewcuts!

Try your luck at one of the following clubs— just a brief guide to where it's all happening: **Count Suckle's Cue Club,** 5a Praed Street, London, W2. **Roaring Sixties,** Carnaby Street, London, W1. **Whisky A Go Go,** Wardour Street, London, W1. **Pink Flamingo,** Wardour Street, London, W1. **Golden Star,** Westbourne Road, London, N7. **Blue Note,** 6a Gore Street, Piccadilly, Manchester. **Savoy Ballrooms,** 73 Rushey Green, London, SE6. **Tottenham Royal,** Tottenham, London, N17. **Apple Tree,** Kingston Hotel, Kingston-on-Thames. **New Century Hall,** Manchester. **Bamboo Club,** 7 St Paul's Street, Bristol. **Concorde,** Bassett Hotel, Burgess Road, Southampton. **Starlite Ballroom,** Allendale Road, Greenford, Middlesex. **The Place,** Victoria Street, Edinburgh. **Marina,** Goldsmith Avenue, Portsmouth.

One of the first discs on the label in the early reggae vein, this was about 30rpm faster than a standard rock steady number! This tells the story of someone (probably producer and ex-associate Joe Gibbs) who makes it big and then turns his back on the people who helped him climb to the top of the pile. Derrick Morgan also used the same rhythm for his *Time Hard* on Crab (CR 28). *People Funny Boy* was also on volume one of *The Trojan Story*.

- *Feel The Rhythm / Easy Snapping*
Clancy Eccles / Theo Beckford
Doctor Bird DB 1156 (1968)
produced by Clancy Eccles
1968 saw Clancy join the new wave of JA producers (Perry, JJ Johnson, Winston Riley et al) who had begun to challenge the supremacy of Duke Reid and Coxsone. This was one of his finest records from that year. Also on Clandisc's *Foolish Fool* compilation.

- **Reggae Prayer / Deliverance Will Come**
Laurel Aitken
Doctor Bird DB 1196 (1969)
produced by Laurel Aitken (UK)
Very much in the style he became famous for, the lyrics are pretty good (read "interesting") too.
This shows why he was still rated as highly as most of his contemporaries, even though his stuff
was recorded away from the West Indies.

- **Heile Heile (The Lion) / Call Collect**
Laurel Aitken / The Seven Letters (aka Symarip)
Doctor Bird DB 1202 (1969)
produced by Laurel Aitken (UK)
Laurel sang about Sellasie years before Rastafarianism came to nationwide attention in the UK,
but the skins never seemed to mind back then. With tunes as good and as danceable as this,
who cared anyway?

Double D

A small independent label apparently run by two brothers, Double D issues are
virtually impossible to find in any condition. Having heard several of them, I can
testify that they're generally above par
rock steady, but definitely give Clive
Bailey's dire *Drink And Drive* a miss.
The label, which was green and yellow
with a picture of the Jamaican national
flag, took the unusual step of noting the
year and month of release on some of its
releases.

The backing outfit on most of the
releases was Bobby Aitken's band, The
Carib-beats, who had a distinctive
"swirling cymbal" type sound. Known
releases were by Bobby himself, Hazel
Wright, The Alpines and Marlene
McKenzie. Such was the level of public
consciousness of this label that, so I'm
told, Bobby Aitken was only told of his
releases on Double D a year or so ago! Without a doubt, the best record I've
heard on the label is Errol Wallace's *Hear My Plea* (DD 109), which is a five star
piece of rock steady. Well worth investigating.

- **Hear My Plea / Unknown Instrumental**
Errol Wallace / The Caribbeats
Double D DD 109 (1968)
producer unknown
A storming piece of rock steady, possibly issued only as a "black label". Wallace cut *Bandit* for
Aston "Family Man" Barrett in '69 which was put out on Escort (ES 817).

Down Town

I've already covered this Trojan / B & C subsidiary in quite a bit of detail in the Dandy UK producer section in one. Basically, the Dandy-produced sides accounted for about 90 out of the label's total output of 120 releases and, while some were good, some were not. After Dandy relinquished production control of Down Town in the early Seventies, the releases covered a hotch-potch of producers and artists.

- ### *Move Your Mule / Reggae Me This, Reggae Me That*
Dandy
Down Town DT 401 (December 1968)
produced by Dandy (UK)
The first on the label and one spin shows why Dandy quickly picked up a sizeable skinhead following. Also on volume one of Down Town's *Red Red Wine* (TTL 11) which also appeared briefly on the Island label.

- ### *Reggae In Your Jeggae / Reggae Shuffle*
Dandy / The Dreamers (but credited to Dandy)
Down Town DT 410 (January 1969)
produced by Dandy (UK)
Cut a good few months earlier than most people realise, this is skinhead reggae par excellence equalling anything coming out of JA at the time. Also on the first volumes of *Red Red Wine* and *Reggae Chartbusters* (in stereo).

- ### *I'm Your Puppet / Water Boy*
Dandy
Down Town DT 416 (March 1969)
produced by Dandy (UK)
A cover of the James And Bobby Purify soul hit which translates really well into reggae. Also on volume one of *Red Red Wine*.

- ### *Red Red Wine / Blues*
Tony Tribe / The Rudies
Down Town DT 419 (April 1969)
produced by Dandy (UK)
A big enough seller to register in the lower rungs of the UK Top 50, legend has it that ol' Tone actually did this on *Top Of The Pops* sporting boots 'n' braces! For someone with such a superbly soulful voice, it's strange that he never recorded more than a handful of 45s (all for Dandy). *Red Red Wine* inspired the two Down Town compilations of the same name and appeared on volume one of *Reggae Chartbusters*. To my mind it's the best version of the song ever recorded (although naturally I'm biased).

- *Tear Them / Chaka Grind*
Desmond Riley / George Lee & The Rudies
Down Town DT 432 (June 1969)
produced by Dandy (UK)
Another skinhead reggae classic which never appeared on any album. It's a pity that so few people will have heard this one as it's an absolute stormer. Des's *Skinhead, A Message To You* (DT 450) is, by contrast, his worst ever record.

- *Burial Of Longshot / Part 2 (Version)*
Prince Of Darkness / George Lee
Down Town DT 441 (1969)
produced by Dandy (UK)
If I had a fiver for every (usually knackered) copy of this I've stumbled across . . . Although completely different from The Pioneers' *Long Shot Kick The Bucket*, it was nevertheless lyrically and topically inspired by it. Dandy himself is probably doing some of the vocals here.

- *Version Girl / Grumble Man*
Boy Friday
Down Town DT 470 (1970)
produced by Dandy (UK)
Just about the last really classic skinhead reggae 45 on Down Town. Boy Friday was the Down Town stable's resident DJ and, as usual, Dandy is in there somewhere. Also on Trojan's second volume of *Club Reggae* (TBL 164).

Duke

Kicking off in November '68, Duke was one of the labels that pre-dated the forming of Trojan / B & C. Early Duke releases by The Techniques (*I Wish It Would Rain*) and The Sensations (*Those Guys*) were Duke Reid productions and should be grabbed with both hands if seen. The label soon covered productions from Clancy Eccles, Lloyd Charmers, Harry J, Winston Riley and Clancy Collins and contained some of Trojan's finest releases from the likes of The Ethiopians (but not *My Girl*!), The Hot Rod All Stars, The Beltones, Carl Dawkins, The Dials and King Cannon (who also went under the names Carl Bryan and Cannonball King). There were brief periods in late '70 and early '71 when the label started to let go of the good quality music with fairly weak UK produced material by the likes of Tony And The Champions, Bill And Pete Campbell and Rupert Cunningham. Otherwise though, this is a label not to be missed.

- *I Wish It Would Rain / There Comes A Time*

The Techniques

Duke DU 1 (November 1968)

produced by Duke Reid

With Pat Kelly on lead vocals, this is a superb early reggae cover of the Temptations' soul classic. Also on Island's ludicrously rare edition of *Tighten Up Volume 2*.

- *Those Guys / I'll Never Fall In Love Again*

The Sensations

Duke DU 2 (December 1968)

produced by Duke Reid

Two great sides from the Duke, the production on these is so crisp and crystal-clear. Top-side was on Island's *Tighten Up Volume 2*. This, and similar Treasure Isle material, should still be available on re-pressed imports, but the quality and mix often leaves a lot to be desired.

- *Cuss Cuss / Lavender Blue*

Lloyd Robinson

Duke DU 5 (January 1969)

produced by Harry J

There was also a horns version of this early reggae vocal by King Cannon (*Soul Special*). Both cuts can be found on Trojan's first compilation LP of Harry Johnson material entitled *No More Heartaches* (TTL 14).

- *Auntie Lu Lu / Bag-A-Boo*

Clancy Eccles / The Slickers

Duke DU 9 (1969)

produced by Clancy Eccles

Both cuts did equally well, Clancy's side being very subtle rude reggae which also found its way onto his *Freedom* LP set on Clandisc.

DU-69 A

THE LAW (Part 1)
ANDY CAPP
Produced by: Byron Lee

B&C Music
℗ 1970

- *John Public (Tom Hark) / Fire Corner*

The Dynamites / King Stitt

Duke DU 30 (June 1969)

produced by Clancy Eccles

The B side did much better and is now regarded as a "talkover" classic. It was a dead cert for inclusion on *Tighten Up Volume 2* and also found its way onto Clandisc's *Fire Corner* compilation.

- *Elizabethan Reggae / Soul Serenade*

Boris Gardner / Winston Wright And The Dragonaires

Duke DU 39 (1969)

produced by Byron Lee

Again, *Elizabethan Reggae* was never intended as the top side but did much bigger business getting as far as number 14 in the UK charts. It was also put out on Doctor Bird's JJ label (DB 1205), but practically all the sales were on Duke. Album-wise, it found its way onto volume one of *Reggae Chartbusters*. Some pressings don't credit Gardner and some do.

- **Love Is A Treasure / I Want To Be**

The Dials / The Diamonds

Duke DU 46 (1969)

produced by Clancy Collins (UK)

Fast and jerky, this one had the same sort of echoey feel present on JA recordings but usually sadly lacking on UK ones. No compilation LP of Sir Collins' material was ever issued by Trojan so this is unavailable on any album. It has nothing to do with the song of the same name done for Duke Reid by Freddy McKay (see Trojan listing later). The band on the flip aren't related to the Jamaican (Mighty) Diamonds but were just one among several of Collins' session outfits.

- **The Law / Instrumental Version**

Andy Capp / Winston Wright & The Dragonaires

Duke DU 69 (1970)

produced by Byron Lee

A subtle "Spaghetti Western" inspired 45 with prominent organ backing courtesy of Winston Wright. Now regarded as a skinhead classic, this was also on *Club Reggae Volume 1* (TBL 159) and Byron Lee And The Dragonaires' *Reggae Blast Off* (TBL 110).

- **Remember That Sunday / Last Lick**

Alton Ellis (With Phyllis Dillon) / Tommy McCook And The Supersonics

Duke DU 72 (1970)

produced by Duke Reid

Probably one of the last tracks Alton cut for the Duke. Also on Trojan's *Reggae, Reggae, Reggae* compilation LP (TBL 130). The flip was an instrumental version of The Sensations' *Those Guys*.

Duke Reid

This was Trojan / B & C's exclusive outlet for Duke Reid productions and is best known for its classic U Roy releases such as *Wake The Town*, *Rule The Nation* and *Wear You To The Ball*. Other artists included Alton Ellis, The Ethiopians, Hopeton Lewis and The Tennors. The last few releases from '73 are not so hot, but on the whole there was hardly a duff issue on this short run of just two dozen 45s.

- **Wake The Town / Big Boy And Teacher (aka What Is Katty)**

U Roy

Duke Reid DR 2509 (1970)

produced by Duke Reid

This DJ version of Alton Ellis' *Girl I've Got A Date* kicked off an extremely successful run of singles for ace DJ, U Roy (real name Ewart Beckford). Released around the late summer of '70, this disc and its successors also inspired a host of imitators and bona-fide challengers for his DJ crown. Both sides can also be found on Trojan's after-the-event hits package, simply titled *U Roy*, put out on its Attack subsidiary in 1974 (ATLP 1006).

- *Rule The Nation / Angle A La La*
U Roy / Nora Dean
Duke Reid DR 2510 (1970)
produced by Duke Reid
This time a talkover version of the Techniques' *Love Is Not A Gamble* issued on UK Treasure Isle (TI 7026) some three years earlier. Another Top Three smash in JA as well.

- *Wear You To The Ball / The Ball (Instrumental Version)*
U Roy / Earl "Wire" Lindo
Duke Reid DR 2513 (1970)
produced by Duke Reid
Bearing the same title as the '67 Paragons' original with John Holt on lead vocals, Trojan put this on *Club Reggae Volume One*. Another biggie.

- *You'll Never Get Away / Rock Away*
U Roy / Tommy McCook Quintet
Duke Reid DR 2514 (1970)
produced by Duke Reid
Was the formula of covering old rock steady tracks wearing a bit thin or was the competition getting a bit fiercer? Difficult to say, but his tour of the UK in '71 still went down a storm. This was a cover of The Melodians' classic of the same name while the flip was an instrumental version of The Sensations' *Everyday Is Just A Holiday* (TR 7701). His last big one in a quartet of ground-breaking 45s.

Dynamic

Another Trojan / B & C label which is still fairly easy to get hold of these days. Its biggest successes came with The Slickers' *Johnny Too Bad*, Eric Donaldson's *Cherry Oh Baby* and *Blue Boot,* and Dennis Alcapone's *Alcapone Guns Don't Bark* and *Ripe Cherry*.

- *Johnny Too Bad / Saucy Horde*
The Slickers / Roland Alphonso
Dynamic DYN 406 (1971)
produced by Byron Lee (for Dynamic Sounds)
As featured in the film, *The Harder They Come*. An early Seventies form of the rude boy theme which found its way onto volume four of the *Tighten Up* series (TBL 163).

Right: Jimmy Cliff who starred in the film, *The Harder They Come*.

78

- **Cherry Oh Baby / Sir Charmers' Special**
Eric Donaldson / Lloyd Charmers
Dynamic DYN 420 (1971)
produced by Byron Lee (for Dynamic Sounds)
1971's Jamaican Song Festival winner, this really established Eric as a solo artist. A big seller that also found a sizeable white audience. Album-wise, also on *Club Reggae Volume 1* and *From Bam Bam To Cherry Oh Baby* (TRL 51).

Escort

A Pama subsidiary, this label initially put out productions by Harry J (some of which strangely appeared on Trojan's *What Am I To Do* compilation album), but then became a mixed bag effort. *What Am I To Do* by Tony Scott was in fact the original vocal cut of the *Liquidator* rhythm and is quite good. Taken as a whole however, Escort lacked the substance of the other Pama labels and apart from such releases as Stranger Cole's *Pretty Cottage*, Sonny Binns' *Boss A Moon* and Slim Smith And The Uniques' original '68 cut of *My Conversation*, there was relatively little worthy of merit here. Pama never issued a *Best Of Escort* compilation, possibly because a lot of the early issues on the label were covered on the aformentioned Trojan LP.

- **Shine Eye Gal / Who Nest (Who's Next)**
Vincent Foster / King Cannon
Escort ES 803 (1969)
produced by Harry J
A short and sweet reggae vocal with King Cannon (real name Carl Bryan) blasting up the rear.

- **What Am I To Do? / Bring Back That Smile**
Tony Scott
Escort ES 805 (1969)
produced by Harry J
The original vocal to *Liquidator*, which was also included on the useful compilation LP of the same name on Harry J (TTL 34).

- **Bossa Moon / Brotherly Love**
S S (Sonny) Binns / Bunny Lee All Stars
Escort ES 818 (1970)
produced by Bunny Lee
An organ cut to Derrick Morgan's *Moon Hop* on Crab with appropriate space noises throughout.

Explosion

This was yet another Trojan / B & C label which began by issuing discs by a certain producer (in this case Derrick Harriott) and diversified shortly thereafter. With the exception of the humdrum *Lemi Li* by Rudy Mills, all the Harriott productions are of a high quality, particularly those by his session band, The Crystalites. There were a few homegrown productions on Dice The Boss and Trevor Lloyd (courtesy of Laurel Aitken), but Alvin Ranglin really put the label on the musical map with the GG All Stars' *Man From Carolina* and *African Melody*, both of which he also sold to Pama! One to avoid is The Maytones' *Another Festival* which was one of their poorer efforts.

- **Death A Come / Zylon**
Lloyd Charmers
Explosion EX 2001 (1969)
produced by Lloyd Charmers
One of his best which was also covered in almost identical fashion by Lloyd Robinson on Crab (CR 27).

- **Chinee Brush / Real Collie**
Trevor Lloyd / (Pama) Dice And Cummie
Explosion EX 2018 (1970)
produced by Laurel Aitken (UK)
Compelling stuff from two-song man Trevor. A real prize in any skinhead's record collection.

- **In The Summertime / Apollo Moon Rock**
Nat Cole
Explosion EX 2022 (1970)
produced by Nat Cole (UK)
In my opinion a better do-over of the Mungo Jerry hit than The Music Doctors' instrumental cut on J-Dan (JDN 4414). The flip's pretty naff though.

- **Man From Carolina / Gold On Your Dress**
The GG All Stars / The Maytones (but credited to GG All Stars)
Explosion EX 2023 (1970)
produced by A Ranglin
One of the most popular reggae instrumentals of that year, this appeared on the compilation album of the same name on GG (TBL 129) and on *Tighten Up Volume 3*. Pama also issued it on their Escort subsidiary (ERT 835) with *African Melody* on the flipside.

- **Skinhead Train / Everstrong**
The Charmers / Tony Binns
Explosion EX 2045 (1971)
produced by Lloyd Charmers
To be perfectly frank, I've never even heard this and twenty years of collecting still hasn't rewarded me with a copy of it. A good reggae vocal, apparently.

Fab

Intended as Melodisc's continuation of the Blue Beat label, Fab issued most of Prince Buster's rock steady output and had an annoying habit of re-using catalogue numbers. As with Blue Beat, Buster's releases consisted of around a third of the label's total output, with the classic *Johnny Cool*, *Shaking Up Orange Street*, *Intensified Dirt*, *Rough Rider* and many, many more. There were a few duffers though by the likes of P J Proby, Phase Four, Sugar Simone, The Minstrels and Jackie Riding, whose *The Wave* is one of the worst records I have ever had the misfortune to hear.

The Buster discs tended to be Fab's bread and butter and after his releases began to dry up around '71, the label issued material by various producers (many of which were on white labels) and completely lost its direction. Taken as a whole, Fab's reputation largely rests on its Buster output and it's his Fab LPs that are most attractive to collectors. Most of these were re-pressed at the height of the Two Tone era and you should beware of dealers trying to pass these off as originals. Generally speaking, the re-issues had very shiny vinyl and "smooth" labels while originals had rougher "papery" ones. I'm quite certain about all this as my copy of *She Was A Rough Rider* was bought from London's Virgin Megastore in 1980 and no way was it an original!

- **Shaking Up Orange Street (aka Sweet P) / Black Girl**
Prince Buster And The All Stars
Fab FAB 10 (1967)
produced by Prince Buster
Utilising the same rhythm as The Tennors' *Pressure And Slide* on Coxsone, this was one of the Prince's earliest and best rock steady efforts.

- *Johnny Cool / Part 2*
Prince Buster And The All Stars
Fab FAB 11 (1967)
produced by Prince Buster
For atmosphere and a superb bass line, this has to be his greatest rock steady ever. Never put out on any album.

- *Rough Rider / 127 Orange Street*
Prince Buster And The All Stars / Buster's All Stars
Fab FAB 40 (1968)
produced by Prince Buster
The Prince was particularly good at rude reggae and rock steady things like this. Also on *Fabulous Greatest Hits*, *She Was A Rough Rider* (BBLP 820) and *Wreck A Pum Pum* (BBLP 821). The last two were on Fab despite the Blue Beat catalogue numbers.

- *Wine And Grind / The Scorcher*
Prince Buster And The All Stars
Fab FAB 81, later re-issued on FAB 108 (1968 and 1969)
produced by Prince Buster
Two blistering fast reggae sides. *Wine And Grind* was also put on the *She Was A Rough Rider*, *Wreck A Pum Pum* and *Big Five* (MI2-157) LP sets.

- *Bull Buck / One Heart (aka Happy Reggae)*
Prince Buster And The All Stars / Roland Alphonso
Fab FAB 118 (1969)
produced by Prince Buster
A long-time skinhead fave which completely missed out in the album stakes.

Gas

The Theo Beckford Group's *The Horse* launched this Pama subsidiary and was a massive club hit at the end of '68. An infectious instrumental, which was actually credited on the label to the producer, Eric Barnet, this disc was in virtually every West Indian household when I was a kid. Other influential Gas releases were Slim Smith And The Uniques' powerful reading of The Temptations' *Ain't Too Proud To Beg*, Martin Riley's *Walking Proud* and Pat Kelly's *How Long Will It Take*, *Festival Time* and *If It Don't Work Out*. Pat's discs definitely need checking out, and *How Long Will It Take* was such a big seller that it still turns up quite frequently these days. A *Gas Greatest Hits* compilation LP was also put out. Like some of the other Pama labels, the quality control system seemed to go on strike in the final stages of the label's run and it's really the '69 issues that command the most attention.

Opposite page: Pat Kelly, London, 1988 (photo by Maverick)

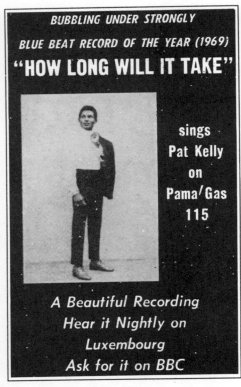

BUBBLING UNDER STRONGLY

BLUE BEAT RECORD OF THE YEAR (1969)

"HOW LONG WILL IT TAKE"

sings
Pat Kelly
on
Pama/Gas
115

A Beautiful Recording
Hear it Nightly on
Luxembourg
Ask for it on BBC

- *The Horse / Action Line*
Theo Beckford's Group (but credited to producer Eric Barnet) / The Versatiles
Gas GAS 100 (1968)
produced by Eric Barnet
A rave record at the time which also had some success in the white discos. On *Reggae Hits '69 Volume 1*. The flip was the first in a run of tunes on a "phone-in radio station" theme.

- *1,000 Tons Of Megaton / Musical Ressurection*
Roland Alphonso
Gas GAS 112 (1969)
produced by Derrick Morgan
A horns version of Slim Smith's *Everybody Needs Love* on Unity. Also on volume one of *Hits '69* and *Gas Greatest Hits* (ECO 4). Don't be without this one. The flip is a rousing version of the *Skokiaan* rhythm.

- *Walking Proud / Why Baby*
Martin Riley / Lloyd Charmers
Gas GAS 114 (1969)
produced by Martin Riley / Lloyd Charmers
A truly great song which could've been a mite better with a beefier backing. Riley's got a superb voice though. On *Gas Greatest Hits*.

- *How Long Will It Take? / Try To Remember*
Pat Kelly
Gas GAS 115 (June 1969)
produced by Bunny Lee
A tune so big that it was even advertised in the pages of the national music press. A very big seller in reggae terms and it can also be found on Pama's *Gas Greatest Hits*, *This Is Reggae Volume 1* and *16 Dynamic Reggae Hits*, alongside Pat's debut album *Pat Kelly Sings* (PMLP 12).

- *Too Proud To Beg / Love And Devotion*
Slim Smith And The Uniques
Gas GAS 117 (1969)
produced by Bunny Lee
The vocals on this one could give the Temps a run for their money any day. It was certainly a song very well suited to a reggae arrangement, and Bunny Lee versioned the rhythm time and time again. On *Gas Greatest Hits* and Slim's debut LP, *Everybody Needs Love* (ECO 9). Hard to find on 45 though.

- **If It Don't Work Out / I'm Coming Home**
Pat Kelly
Gas GAS 125 (1969)
produced by Bunny Lee
A reggae cover of The Casino's powerful *Then You Can Tell Me Goodbye* on President, it was also covered by Slim Smith and Joe White. Pat's version was put on his *Sings* album and *A Gift From Pama*.

- **Ba Ba / Power Cut**
The Slickers / Glen Adams
Gas GAS 135 (1969)
produced by Lee Perry / Glen Adams
Actually the same as *What Is This?* by The Reggae Boys which was on the *Clint Eastwood* album (PSP 1014). Great Lee Perry stuff. The flip is practically the same as The Upsetters' *Cold Sweat*, but without the spoken intro.

GG

This was Trojan / B & C's exclusive outlet for Alvin Ranglin productions from '70-'73, after which it went independent and survived well into the late Seventies. There was quite a lot of ethnic material on this label like Max Romeo And Glen Brown's *Jordan River*, Gerald McKlish's *False Reaper* and The Maytones' *Cleanliness*, which were not particularly skinhead-friendly, but nonetheless contained some very hard rhythms. On the positive side, all the Charlie Ace DJ releases are good, as is The Ethiopians' *Sound Of Our Forefathers / Love Bug* which also came out on Pama's Supreme subsidiary. The record that really broke the label was Verne And Son's *Little Boy Blue* which can also be found on volume two of Trojan's *Club Reggae* series.

- **Feel It (More And More) / It's Been A Long Time**
Paulette & Gee (aka The Ebony Sisters) / Winston Wright
GG GG 4504 (1970)
produced by A Ranglin
Also put out on Camel under the name of *Sister* (CA 55) and included on Pama's *This Is Reggae Volume 2* (PMP 2005). Winston Wright's straight organ version on the flip was in fact the A side and is also good.

- **Do Something / Groove Me**
Charley Ace / The Maytones
GG GG 4518 (1971)
produced by A Ranglin
Talkover star Mr Ace (who recorded for Joe Gibbs under the banner Johnny Lover) had a good line in patter and this one's worth a listen. His *Ontarius Version* (GG 4507) is a DJ version of Paulette & Gee's *Feel It*, and is also well worth a spin. *Do Something* was also issued on Pama's Punch label (PH 67) and their *Hot Numbers Volume 1* compilation (PMP 2006).

Giant

Stamford Hill record shop owners Rita and Benny King have already been mentioned several times in this book and added Giant to their empire in '67 with Dandy very much in mind. He produced and / or sung on 26 of the label's total of 39 issues and some of his rock steady outings are quite good, particularly *Sweet Ride*. There were a few non-UK efforts by Roy Shirley (*Dance Arena* and *Warming Up The Scene*), Pat Kelly And The Uniques (the timeless *Little Boy Blue*) and an obscure vocalist by the name of Albert Tomlinson (*Don't Wait For Me*, which is very good indeed). Unplayed copies of Giant releases are still relatively easy to get hold of, largely because Rita and Benny apparently sold off all their unsold

stock when they closed down their shop in the early Eighties to return to JA. There was just one LP issue on the label, Dandy's *Rock Steady With Dandy*, which has long been very collectable.

- ***Keep On Fighting / Rock Steady Boogie***
Don Martin And The Superboys / The Superboys
Giant GN 24 (1968)
produced by Dandy (UK)
A truly great "sufferers" song from the unknown Don. Probably the best UK recording ever put out on the label.

- ***Dance Hall Arena / Musical Train***
Roy Shirley & The Caribbeats
Giant GN 32 (1968)
produced by Bunny Lee
One of the relatively few JA recordings on Giant, *Musical Train* was later put on *The Trojan Story Volume 1*. Relegated to the flip side here, it was nonetheless the better of the two.

- ***Warming Up The Scene / Hey There Lonely Girl***
Roy Shirley / Glen Adams
Giant GN 33 (1968)
produced by Bunny Lee
Another stormer from Roy. The rhythm was used in '72 for The Deltones' *Tropical Lament* to be found on volume two of Trojan's *Music House* series of compilation albums (TBL 177).

- ***A Change Gonna Come / Jumping With Val***
Ken Parker / Val Bennett
Giant GN 34 (1968)
produced by Bunny Lee
Amazing how certain labels put out a consecutive run of 45s from a certain producer, this being the last in a trio of Giant singles from Bunny Lee. Actually a cover of a song by Sam Cooke, who had long been a favourite with West Indian audiences.

Gayfeet

A Trojan / B & C label that dealt with Sonia Pottinger productions, only 12 issues were put out during two shortlived series ('69-'70 and '73). The seven issues that came out in the label's first phase are generally hard to find, except Junior Soul's (later known as Murvin) *Jennifer / Slipping* which was a sizeable reggae chart hit and is worth a second glance. The second series spawned just one decent issue, namely Big Youth's *Medicine Doctor / Facts Of Life*.

Grape

A Trojan / B & C label, this outlet began in '69 by issuing 100% UK productions - including some first-rate skinhead reggae by the likes of J Sinclair (on Freddie Notes And The Rudies) and Laurel Aitken (on King Horror). The best way to get hold of the Horror sides is to track down Trojan's *Lochness Monster* compilation LP which contains his title track (which was very popular at the time), *Cutting Blade* and the very rude *The Hole*. In fact, *Lochness Monster* was one of those relatively few UK recorded singles which successfully crossed over to the West Indian market in a big way. The most talked about single from Grape's initial batch of releases is Claudette's *Skinheads A Bash Dem*, which I have neither heard nor seen for sale since I first heard of its existence in a letter in one of the national papers nearly 20 years ago. So there.

The other way to pick up some of the early Grape issues is to find a copy of Trojan's *Queen Of The World* compilation (TBL 136) which includes Des All Stars, Johnny Youth and good old Winston Groov(e)y himself. Grape's first phase finished at around the same time Trojan called time on its other labels issuing 100% UK-product like Joe and Hot Rod, but was resurrected in '72 to become a mixed-producer label putting out mostly JA recorded releases by Dennis Alcapone, Big Youth, Freddy McKay and Alton Ellis.

- **Cutting Blade / The Vampire**
King Horror
Grape GR 3003 (1969)
produced by Laurel Aitken (UK)
As rude-as-they-come (no pun intended) slab of skinhead reggae which was also put out on Trojan's classic *Lochness Monster* compilation LP of mainly UK productions (TBL 135).

- **Lochness Monster / Zion I**
King Horror
Grape GR 3007 (1969)
produced by Laurel Aitken (UK)
Largely an instrumental, with Reco Rodriguez blasting away in the background. A very big seller for a UK production which gave rise to the title of Trojan's compilation.

- *See-Through Craze / I'm The One*
Roy Smith / Teddy, Carl And Derrick
Grape GR 3013 (1970)
produced by Calva L (Les) Foster (UK)
A very hard to find rude reggae 45 with a sparse bass 'n' drums rhythm.

- *Skinheads A Bash Them / Walking Thru' Jerusalem*
Claudette And The Corporation
Grape GR 3020 (1970)
produced by Laurel Aitken (UK)
One of the classic made-for-the-skinhead-market records. Copies have now completely dried up due to over-subscribed collector interest and on the very rare occasions it does get offered for sale its always up for grabs on a "highest bid wins" basis. If you're lucky, you just might get to hear it on a mate's tape.

Green Door

A Trojan / B & C label, Green Door tended to put out rootsy tracks by the likes of The Charmers, The Wailing Souls and Bob Marley And The Wailers. The label is however most notable for its superb array of DJ sides from I Roy, U Roy, Lloyd Young, Dennis Alcapone, Shorty The President and Big Youth.

Harry J

This was Trojan / B & C's exclusive outlet for Harry Johnson productions and is most famous for its two UK chart hits, namely Bob and Marcia's *Young, Gifted And Black* and Harry J All Stars' *Liquidator*. Other artists on Harry J were Bob Andy, Busty Brown, The Jay Boys (who also doubled up as The Harry J All Stars), The Cables and Blake Boy (alias organist and JA producer Winston Blake). You can actually pick up large chunks of the earliest cuts ('70) on the label by getting hold of two of Harry J's compilation LPs, *The Liquidator* (containing tracks by the Harry J All Stars and The Jay Boys) and *Reggae Movement*.

A lot of Harry J material tends to be a bit on the commercial side and its releases are not generally as sought after as some of Trojan's other labels. One of the most favourable 45s on Harry J however is DJ Lizzy's *More Heartaches*, which was a cut to the Beltones' *No More Heartaches*. The label soldiered on until '74 with plenty of naff reggae versions of pop songs of the day like *Rock Your Baby*, *Walking Miracle* and *Kung Fu Fighting*, but a year or two prior to this Harry J really did put out some decent stuff. Carey and Lloyd's *Down Side Up* (credited to the Harry J All Stars on the label), I Roy's *Musical Drum Sound* and The Ethiopians' *The Word Is Love* from '72-'73 really did the business, albeit after the skinheads.

- *Liquidator / La La Always Stay (aka Rich In Love)*
Harry J All Stars / Glen (Adams) And Dave (Barker)
Harry JTR 675 (1969)
produced by Harry Johnson
With Winston Wright on organ, this instrumental version of Tony Scott's *What Am I To Do* (see Escort label) was a massive UK hit towards the end of '69. Also on Trojan's Harry J label LP of the same name (TBL 104) and *Reggae Chartbusters Volume 1*. Some earlier green label copies had The Jay Boys' *Festive Spirit* as the flip side.

High Note

Like Blue Cat, High Note's earliest sides have become very rare these days. As Trojan / B & C's principal outfit for Sonia Pottinger productions (the other was Gayfeet), the label put out around 60 singles between '68 and '72 by the likes of The Gaylads, Ken Boothe, The Beltones, The Hippy Boys, and Delano Stewart. There were a few excellent LPs released too like The Hippy Boys' *Reggae With The Hippy Boys*, a dual artist album by Lynn Tait and Roland Alphonso entitled, *ABC Rock Steady*, and a various artists effort called *Dancing Down Orange Street*. As

a session band, The Hippy Boys probably had a fairly fluid line-up, but it is known that Glen Adams and other members of The Upsetters (also in fact a session band) played on a number of Hippy Boys' tracks.

There are plenty of scorchers on High Note, but the most listenable to my mind are Patsy's *We Were Lovers* (a do-over of a soul track), Delano Stewart's *Got To Come Back*, and The Gaytones' *Ten To One* with Busty Brown on vocals. After 1970, Pottinger's productions tended to lose their rough edge, but High Note certainly turned out some very consistent material over the first two of its four year existence.

- **We Were Lovers / Give Me A Chance**
Patsy Todd / Patsy And Delano Stewart
High Note HS 012 (February 1969)
produced by Sonia Pottinger
Careful to turn this one down or you'll have no ears left! Great song, superbly sung by sweet-voiced Patsy.

- **Reggae Buddy / Easy Squeeze**
The Victors
High Note HS 019 (1969)
produced by Sonia Pottinger
Nice "easy ride" reggae, a pity this band weren't heard more in the UK.

- **Got To Come Back / Don't Believe Him**
Delano Stewart
High Note HS 027 (1969)
produced by Sonia Pottinger
Anything by Delano on High Note is well above par, but this one's particularly tasty. Great bass line, which Laurel Aitken used for his *Got To Have Your Love* on Newbeat (NB 049). On Delano's *Stay A Little Bit Longer* LP on High Note (TBL 138) and Trojan's *Reggae, Reggae, Reggae* compilation (TBL 130).

- *Stay A Little Bit Longer / Version*

Delano Stewart / The Hippy Boys

High Note HS 041 (1970)

produced by Sonia Pottinger

Better than Larry Marshall's Studio One cut on Banana (BA 300). A beautiful record also put out on his album of the same name and Tighten Up volume 3. The Hippy Boys were on the flip and, as a footnote, their stuff on High Note, like *Dr. No Go* and *Reggae Pressure*, is also well worth picking up.

- *Ten To One / Another Version*

The Gaytones (with Busty Brown on vocals) / The Gaytones

High Note HS 048 (1970)

produced by Sonia Pottinger

Also put out on Escort as *Man Short* with Dave Barker And The Gaylads' great *She Want It* on the flip (which also saw release on High Note HS 049!). A bit calypso-ish, this was on the census taker theme - yet another short-lived "current affairs" topic in JA at the time which was immortalised in the music.

Hillcrest

One of R & B Discs later subsidiaries, Hillcrest put out just seven 45s between '71 and '72. King Cannon's *Reggae Got Soul* was also put out on Junior and is highly recommended. That, and Glen Adams' rare *The Lion Sleeps* are the only two tracks I've heard on this hard to come by label.

Horse

Originally intended as a pop label, Trojan's Horse subsidiary is best known for its two Dandy Livingstone chart hits. Otherwise, there's nothing to commend it whatsoever as most of its releases came after the skinheads and tended to be very much at the commercial end of reggae. Look out however for Winston Wright's *Soul Serenade / Bond In Bliss* which were both re-issues from the Duke and Trojan labels respectively.

Hot Lead

This one's a real mystery. The only issues I can ever remember seeing were by Mr T Bones (whoever he was) and Inner Mind, who cut some sides for various Pama subsidiaries with a guy called Ian Smith at the mixing desk. If memory serves correct (!) the label emanated from Yorkshire and, as such, may not have received very wide distribution.

TROJAN TOP 40

TOP 40

1	PAPA WAS A ROLLING STONE	SIDNEY, GEORGE & JACKIE	ATT 8054
2	CHECK OUT YOURSELF	CIMARONS	TR 7890
3	BIG EIGHT	JUDGE DREAD	BI.619
4	BUILD IT UP	TITO SIMON	HOSS 30
5	IMAGES OF YOU	NICKY THOMAS	HOSS 29
6	COME BACK LIZA	DANDY LIVINGSTONE	HOSS 28
7	SEVEN LITTLE GIRLS	PEACHES	EX.2081
8	MULTIPLICATION	THOROUGHBREDS	ATT.8049
9	TON-UP KIDS	DAVE & ANSEL COLLINS	TR 7891
10	ONE WOMAN	BOB ANDY	HOSS.31
11	LOUIE LOUIE	THE MAYTALS	TR 7865
12	YOU CAN'T BUY MY LOVE/		
	THE FIRST CUT IS THE DEEPEST	DONNA DAWSON	TR.7892
13	NICE ONE CYRIL	BREADCRUMBS	ATT.8051
14	GUNS OF NAVARONE/		
	BONANZA SKA	SKATALITES	TRM.9008
15	DING-A-LING TING-A-LING	STEVE COLLINS	BI.620.
16	HAVE A LITTLE FAITH	NICKY THOMAS	TR.7885
17	WHAT ABOUT YOU	PAT RHODEN	TR 7889
18	AT THE DISCOTHEQUE	THE PIONEERS	TR 7888
19	ALONE AGAIN, NATURALLY	NOW GENERATION	GD.4055
20	LONELY SOLDIER	GREGORY ISAACS	GD.4054
21	SILVER WORDS	KEN BOOTHE	GD.4053
22	YOU DON'T KNOW	BOB ANDY	GD.4059
23	BIG SEVEN	JUDGE DREAD	BI.613
24	GIVE ME A CHANCE	THE CABLES	ATT.8053
25	GIVE ME LOVE	CORNELL CAMPBELL	GD.4057
26	SPACE FLIGHT	I. ROY	ATT.8050
27	BIG SIX	JUDGE DREAD	BI 608
28	BIG ELEVEN	DERRICK MORGAN	ATT 8048
29	THE FURTHER YOU LOOK	JOHN HOLT	HOSS.22
30	THE TIME HAS COME	SLIM SMITH	EX 2074
31	SHA LA LA LA LEE	CLEMENT BUSHEY	EX.2082
32	DON'T THROW STONES	SYDNEY ROGER'S FIGHTERS	BI.621
33	TIME AND THE RIVER	JOHN HOLT	ATT.8045
34	IS IT BECAUSE I'M BLACK	KEN BOOTHE	TR.7893
35	LET ME LOVE YOU	SLIM SMITH	GD.4058
36	LOVING HER WAS EASY	LLOYD CHALMERS	HOSS.32
37	EVERYBODY PLAYS THE FOOL	THE CHOSEN FEW	TR.7882
38	IT'S NOT WHO YOU KNOW	THE TWINKLE BROTHERS	BI.600
39	AIN'T THAT PECULIAR	DELROY WILSON	GD.4060
40	NICE, NICE TIME	ZAP POW	TR.7886

ARTIST OF THE MONTH
NICKY THOMAS
ALBUMS
TBL.143 Love of the Common People
TRLS.25 Tell It Like It is
SINGLES
TR.7885 Have A Little Faith
HOSS.29 Images OF You

DISCO SPOT
SHA LA LA LA LEE
SHA LA LA LA LEE – CLEMENT BUSHEY EX. 2082
Dance-sing-along time with the Bubble Reggae
version of old Small Faces hit.

NEW RELEASES
W/E 13 JULY 1973

BROWN BABY	DERRICK HARRIOTT	ATT.8056
REGGAE MAKOSSA	BRENT DOWE	GD.4061
I'M A BELIEVER	WINSTON TUCKER	EX.2083
LIVE TO LOVE	SID COOK	ATT.8055
AM I BLACK ENOUGH!	CHOSEN FEW	TR.7894

PICK OF
THE WEEK
AM I BLACK ENOUGH!
CHOSEN FEW TR 7894
Talented Chosen Few Best Ever. Funk Reggae
styling of Soul. This MUST go National Chart- wise.

STOP PRESS: WHERE TO SEE YOUR FAVOURITE TROJAN ARTISTS
DANDY LIVINGSTONE
July 29th – Wolverhampton. Aug. 18th – Bedford. Aug. 25th – Hastings. Aug. 27th – Bristol.
MARVELS
July 7th – Empire Rooms, London. July 26th – Oldham. Aug. 3rd – Nottingham. Aug. 27th – Liverpool.
PIONEERS
July 8th – Wolverhampton. July 21st – Huddersfield. Aug. 18th – Ely. Aug. 25th – Hastings. Aug. 27th – Bristol.
NICKY THOMAS
July 14th – Luton/Gloucester. July 22nd – Kent. July 27th – Leicester. Aug. 4th – London. Aug. 25th – Hastings. Aug. 27th – Wolverhampton.
CIMARONS
July 6th – Brent Town Hall, London. July 20th – Bristol (Top Rank). Aug. 00th – Bath (Pavillion). Aug. 26th (Darby Ray – Bristol.

AVAILABLE FROM EMI, LUGTONS, TAYLORS & TROJAN SALES

91

Hot Rod

Trojan / B & C's outlet for Lambert Briscoe productions, Hot Rod boasted one of the better "Made For Skinheads" records of the period with the Hot Rod All Stars' *Skinhead Speaks His Mind*. The label was also responsible for putting out Tony Nash's *Keep on Trying* which, although a commercial effort with strings 'n' things, was a good tune nonetheless. Oddly enough, Trojan never put a single Hot Rod cut on any of its compilation LPs, while most of its other subsidiaries all had at least one track put out on this format - some, like Joe, even had entire LPs devoted to them. Largely because they are almost completely unobtainable- in any shape or form - people are paying extortionate prices for old Hot Rod 45s these days. Come on Trojan, what about some re-issues?

• *Skinhead Speaks His Mind / Carnaby Street*
Hot Rod All Stars / Carl Levy
Hot Rod HR 104 (1970)
produced by Lambert Briscoe (UK)
For skinhead reggae, Hot Rod really did the business. This was another "quality" record made for the skinheads which is now a big money item. Carl Levy on the flip was organist with The Cimarrons.

• *Strictly Invitation / Dog Your Woman*
Patsy And Peggy
Hot Rod HR 107 (1970)
produced by Lambert Briscoe (UK)
Again, top-notch skinhead reggae, with a nice rude one on the flip. Peggy also cut a naff version of *All Kinds Of Everything* for Joe Sinclair on Trojan.

• *Keep On Trying / Just Can't Do Without Your Love*
Tony Nash / Winston James
Hot Rod HR 110 (1970)
produced by Lambert Briscoe (UK)
A good piece of UK commercial reggae for a change, with strings and all. Quite soulful too. Makes you wonder what happens to all those singers who only put out one tune.

Hot Shot

Just one issue has ever come to my attention on this Torpedo offshoot, namely Nehemia Reid All Stars' *Hot Pepper / Sea Wave*, both of which were fairly good instrumentals. As this disc actually had the number HS 03, there were probably other releases too. Reid was in fact originally a solo vocalist who cut *The Fiddle* (issued on Blue Cat) and *Family War* (issued on Island) in '68.

Island

Chris Blackwell's Island label virtually had the monopoly on the UK ska and rock steady market come '66 and '67. As with Doctor Bird, most of Jamaica's most popular artists had records put out on Island, namely Derrick Morgan, The Gaylads, The Wailers, Slim Smith, The Tartans, Lee Perry, and Jackie Mittoo And The Soul Brothers. The list is quite phenomenal, and its roster of producers took in Coxsone Dodd, Leslie Kong, Derrick Harriott, Bunny Lee and Duke Reid, among others. The practice of one label putting out material by so many different producers was effectively aborted after Trojan became an independent company and began setting up specific subsidiaries dealing with the output of most of the major JA producers.

Island also led the way in ska and rock steady albums, which were otherwise relatively few and far between at the time. Almost all Island's early ('64-'68) LPs, whether they be by more middle-of-the-road artists like Keith And Enid, Jackie Edwards or Joyce Bond, all fetch prices in excess of £30 these days. The most sought after however are the compilations such as *Club Ska '67*, *Club Rock*

Steady, *Put It On* and *Leaping With Mr (Bunny) Lee*, as well as Derrick Harriott and Hopeton Lewis's solo efforts. Trojan did the decent thing in 1970 and re-issued most of them, but these pressings are even harder to find now than the Island originals!

By 1967, Island was enjoying success in the rock and psychedelic field with Traffic and was trying to shed its reputation as a long-time black music specialist. To its credit, Island continued putting out JA sounds until late '68, leaving Trojan to pick up the mantle from then on.

As for the singles, Island devoted a second series to its mainstream pop and rock releases in '67, but be careful of the odd pop disc on the JA series by the likes of Chords Five, Wynder K Frog, The Circles and Kim Fowley. Otherwise you can't really go wrong.

- *I'm The Toughest / No Faith*
Peter Tosh & The Wailers / Marcia Griffiths
Island WI 3042 (1967)
produced by Coxsone Dodd
Great rude boy rock steady from Peter.

- *On The Beach / Sweet And Gentle*
The Paragons / Tommy McCook
Island WI 3045 (1967)
produced by Duke Reid
The lyrics are a bit trite, but the tune's great. John Holt sang lead with the band at this time. *On The Beach* also appeared on Doctor Bird's incredibly rare album of the same name (DLM 5010).

- **Never Let Me Go / Won't Go Away**
Slim Smith & The Uniques / Henry III
Island WI 3087 (1967)
produced by Bunny Lee / F.R.M.
Slow rock steady at its finest. Simply brilliant. Also available on Slim's *Just A Dream* LP set on Trojan (TBL 186).

- **Stop That Train / Feeling Peckish**
Keith And Tex / Bobby Ellis & The Crystalites
Island WI 3091 (1967)
produced by Derrick Harriott
This was originally a ska tune done by The Spanishtonians on Blue Beat in '65. "Stop that train, I wanna get on, my baby she is leaving me now" go the lyrics. Scotty's DJ version of it, *Draw Your Brakes*, was featured in the film *The Harder They Come,* and this one was the first in two or three classic sides from K & T.

- **Long Story / Now We Know**
Rudy Mills / Bobby Ellis & The Crystalites
Island WI 3092 (1967)
produced by Derrick Harriott
Nice one, Rudy. Still played a lot today on the "revival" pirate radio shows, this was his first big seller coming a year or so before *John Jones.* Also on his Pama LP.

- **My Conversation / Love One Another**
Slim Smith And The Uniques / Slim Smith
Island WI 3122 (1968)
produced by Bunny Lee
Lee used the rhythm from this solid gold rock steady classic again and again. Even Rupie Edwards used it at one point! Fortunately, it's been continuously available for the past twenty or so years as a track on Slim's *Memorial* set on Trojan (TBL 198). Escort also put it out as a flipside to a current cut from Slim in '71 (ERT 852).

- **Penny For Your Song / I've Passed This Way Before**
The Federals
Island WI 3126 (1968)
produced by Derrick Harriott
Scotty of later DJ fame was on lead vocals here and re-cut it again in reggae style in '71 (Song Bird SB 1056). The original was on Trojan's *Ride Your Donkey* compilation of Island material (TTL 18).

- **Ride Your Donkey / I've Got To Get You Off My Mind**
The Tennors
Island WI 3133 (1968)
produced by A G Murphy
Put out on Fab too under the title *Cleopatra* (Fab 41), this sold particularly well and is now regarded as a late rock steady classic. Also on Trojan's LP of the same name.

- *Hold You Jack / One Morning In May*
Derrick Morgan
Island WI 3159 (November 1968)
produced by Bunny Lee
The penultimate single on Island, and one of the very few reggae sides issued on the label. By this time, Trojan and its subsidiaries had almost completely subsumed anything that would formerly have been issued on Island. *Hold You Jack* was the first track to use the famous *Wet Dream* rhythm and was also put out on Derrick's *Seven Letter* album on Trojan (TTL 5) and the *Ride Your Donkey* set.

Symarip . . . No. 11 and going down !

SKA & REGGAE

TOP 20 SINGLES

1	1	THE LIQUIDATOR: Harry J's All Stars: Trojan 675 (3)
3	2	SWEET SENSATION: The Melodians: Trojan 695 (3)
2	3	MOON HOP: Derrick Morgan: Crab 32 (3)
4	4	PICKNEY GIRL: Desmond Dekker: Pyramid 6070 (3)
8	5	ELISABETHAN REGGAE: Byron Lee: Duke 39 (3)
13	6	REGGAE PRESSURE: The Hippy Boys: High Note 035 (2)
5	7	WONDERFUL WORLD, BEAUTIFUL PEOPLE: Jimmy Cliff: Trojan 690 (3)
6	8	RETURN OF DJANGO: The Upsetters: Upsetter 301 (3)
14	9	PRESSURE DROP: The Maytals: Trojan 7709 (2)
	10	SHANGHAI: Freddie Notes & the Rudies: Trojan 7713 (1)
7	11	SKINHEAD MOON STOMP: Symarip: Treasure Isle 7050 (3)
12	12	POP A TOP: Andy Capp: Treasure Isle 7052 (3)
	13	MOONLIGHT GROOVER: Winston Wright: Trojan 7701 (1)
	14	CLINT EASTWOOD: The Upsetters: Punch 21 (1)
	15	LOCK JAW: Tommy & the Upsetters: Trojan 7717 (1)
9	16	POOR RAMESES: The Pioneers: Trojan 698 (3)
11	17	LONG SHOT (KICK THE BUCKET): The Pioneers: Trojan 672 (3)
	18	EASE UP: The Bleechers: Trojan 679 (1)
10	19	GIRL WHAT ARE YOU DOING TO ME: Owen Gray: Camel 25 (3)
	20	LET'S GO STEADY MY LOVE: Erroll Daniels: MCA 5025 (1)

TOP 10 ALBUMS

1 TIGHTEN UP VOL. 2: Various Artists: Trojan TTL 7 (3)
2 RED RED WINE: Various Artists: Trojan TTL 11 (3)
3 TIGHTEN UP VOL. 1: Various Artists: Trojan TTL 1 (3)
4 REGGAE POWER: The Ethiopians: Trojan TTL 10 (3)
5 JIMMY CLIFF: Trojan TRLS 16 (2)
6 THE UPSETTER: Various Artists: Trojan TTL 13 (3)
7 GUNS OF NAVARONE: Various Artists: Trojan TTL 16 (3)
8 REGGAE SPECIAL: Various Artists: Coxsone 2 (3)
9 THIS IS DESMOND DEKKER: Trojan TTL 4 (3)
10 FIRE CORNER: The Dynamites: Trojan TTL 21 (2)

Jackpot

This was Trojan / B & C's outlet for Bunny Lee productions, although there were brief periods early on in the series when it dealt with UK productions by Laurel Aitken, Nat Cole and Larry Lawrence and a couple of lesser-known JA production men like Phil Pratt and Melmouth Nelson. The first record on Jackpot was Derrick Morgan's *Seven Letters*, and sported a plain mustard colour label while later discs had a label design very similar to the label's JA counterpart.

There was some first rate music on Jackpot from Slim Smith, Dave Barker, John Holt, Delroy Wilson and DJ Winston Williams, whose *The People's Choice* and *DJ's Choice* are excellent. Lee covered his tracks on a number of Jackpot sides which he'd also sold to Pama by crediting them to different artists and sometimes even re-titling them. Pat Kelly became Little Boy Blue, and his *Sweeten My Coffee* was in fact *If It Don't Work Out* which also came out on Gas. Similarly, Slim Smith became Wonder Boy and Lester Sterling had releases out on Jackpot under the name Mr Versatile!

Two other points to bear in mind are that Winston Groov(e)y's *Funky Chicken* (JP 708) and Dave Barker's *Sex Machine* (JP 751) aren't covers of the soul tracks done by Rufus Thomas and James Brown respectively, but totally different tunes. Look out in particular for the Dennis Alcapone and Lizzy sides from '71 as Bunny Lee really did a good job with his productions on these two.

- *Seven Letters / Too Bad*
Derrick Morgan
Jackpot JP 700 (1969)
produced by Bunny Lee
This fast-reggae rendition of a Ben E King number was also sold to Trojan's main business rivals Pama who put it out on their Crab subsidiary (CR 8). Also on Derrick's *Seven Letters* Trojan LP and Pama's *In London* set (ECO 10) as well as the company's *Sixteen Dynamic Reggae Hits*.

- *Dark End Of The Street / Apple Blossoms*
Little Boy Blue (Pat Kelly) / Mr Versatile (Lester Sterling)
Jackpot JP 701 (1969)
produced by Bunny Lee
The producer was by this stage using psuedonyms to conceal his artists' identities from respective record companies. This was put out by Pama on the *Pat Kelly Sings* LP and is another great reggae cover of a soul song.

- *Funky Chicken / Version 2*
Winston Groovey / The Cimarrons
Jackpot JP 708 (1970)
produced by Laurel Aitken (UK)
Still quite easy to find these days as it shifted a good few units and was one of sizeable brace of UK-produced 45s put out on Jackpot. Title track of a Trojan compilation too (TBL 137). The flip wasn't in fact a version and is entirely different.

- *Riot / Girls And Boys*
Moffat All Stars / The Impersonators
Jackpot JP 719 (1970)
produced by Melmouth Nelson
A driving organ instrumental, Upsetters style, which is now as rare as hen's teeth.

- *Sugar Sugar / Sign Off*
Nat Cole / Sonny Binns
Jackpot JP 722 (1970)
produced by Nat Cole (UK)
Translated really well into reggae and was on Trojan's *Reggae Reggae Reggae* compilation.

- *DJ's Choice / Can't Do Without It*
Winston Williams/Slim Smith & The Uniques
Jackpot JP 733 (1970)
produced by Bunny Lee
If there was ever a tailor-made DJ for the skinheads, then it has to be "The Aggro Man", Winston Williams. He may have only made a few records, but all of them just bubble over with great patter. Nice rock steady from Slim and the boys on the flip.

- *The People's Choice / Let Me Go Girl*
Winston Williams / Bobby James
Jackpot JP 743 (1970)
produced by Bunny Lee
Great version of Slim and The Uniques' *Ain't Too Proud To Beg*. This one's even better than *DJ's Choice*.

- *Better Must Come / Version*
Delroy Wilson / Bunny Lee All Stars
Jackpot JP 763 (1971)
produced by Bunny Lee
A song which centred on the political struggle in Jamaica during the '71-'72 election, although it was essentially about the underdog fighting back. There were an increasing number of similar songs emanating from JA with a "reality" message during the early Seventies. Also on Del's album of the same name on Trojan (TRL 44) and *Tighten Up Volume 5*.

J-Dan

Already mentioned in chapter one's article on Dandy, J-Dan was something of an overspill label from Down Town. Some of the label's output was good, like George Lee And The Music Doctors' *Johnny Dollar*, which was a horns cut to Dandy's *Raining In My Heart*, and the Mother's Sons' *I Want To Tell The World*. However, this isn't a good one to go in blind, as some of the releases were pretty disappointing.

- *Bush Doctor / Lick Your Stick*
The Music Doctors
J-Dan JDN 4403 (1970)
produced by Dandy (UK)
Without a doubt one of the best instrumentals
ever laid down over in Blighty. Deservedly put
on *Tighten Up Volume 4*.

JJ

 As previously mentioned in the
Doctor Bird label coverage, the JJ label
was intended for productions from JJ
Johnson, but was actually used for discs
by an assortment of producers. JJ
initially used the main Doctor Bird label
catalogue numbers rather than its own
and was primarily devoted (when Doctor Bird got it right!) to The Ethiopians who
were doing big business in '69 with *Everything Crash*, *Hong Kong Flu*, and the
mighty *What A Fire*. All these are classic skinhead cuts not to be missed.

- *That's Life / Tell Me Baby*
Delano Stewart
JJ DB 1138 (1968)
produced by Sonia Pottinger
Delano's first solo disc over here (he was with The Gaylads for a time), it suffers a bit from a
slightly lacklustre backing but is nonetheless still a classic. Also on his *Stay A Little Bit Longer*
album on High Note. Honey Boy re-cut it as *Fight Life* for Count Shelly in '73.

- *Massie Massa / San Sebastian*
The Tennors / Clive's All Stars
JJ DB 1152 (1968)
produced by A G Murphy
The vocal cut to *Donkey Trot* on the flip of The
Tennors' *Girl* on Big Shot.

- *Everything Crash / I'm Not Losing
You*
The Ethiopians
JJ DB 1169 (1968)
produced by JJ Johnson
A reflection of how things were in Jamaica in the
late Sixties. Also on their Trojan albums, *Power*
(TTL 10) and *Woman Capture Man* (TBL 112).

- *Hong Kong Flu / Clap Your Hands*
The Ethiopians
JJ DB 1185 (1969)
produced by JJ Johnson
Another topical number put on both their Trojan LPs and also another big hit.

- *What A Fire / You*
The Ethiopians
JJ DB 1186 (1969)
produced by JJ Johnson
As with all The Ethiopians' JJ Johnson produced material, this had really powerful backing from session band the JJ All Stars. Also on *Power*.

- *The Rise And Fall (Of Laurel Aitken) / If You're Not Black*
Laurel Aitken
JJ DB 1197 (1969)
produced by Laurel Aitken & Graeme Goodall for Bird Music (UK)
Good rude which, rhythm-wise, slightly lacks the hard edge of his best Nu-Beat sides.

- *Scare Him / In My Heart*
The Maytals
JJ PYR 6064 (1968)
produced by Leslie Kong
Hard ethnic early reggae. They also cut this one for Coxsone Dodd as The Flames. The flip was in a slow soul vein.

Joe
One of the all-time classic skinhead labels and already mentioned several times in this book. What more can I say?

- *Dracula Prince Of Darkness / Honky*
King Horror / Joe's All Stars
Joe DU 34 (1969)
produced by Joe Mansano (UK)
Hammer horror reggae also on the *Lochness Monster* compilation.

- *Brixton Cat / Solitude*
Dice The Boss / Joe's All Stars
Joe DU 50 (1969)
produced by Joe Mansano (UK)
Popular enough for Trojan to put out the *Brixton Cat* compilation of Mansano material (TBL 106). Brit-produced stuff had become big business for reggae companies by this time and this one did pretty well for Trojan. I picked up a copy of it with a load of other more common skinhead reggae stuff in a South coast second-hand shop back in the late Seventies, so it must've travelled pretty well too!

- *Your Boss DJ / Read The News*
Dice The Boss / Tito Simon
Joe DU 57 (1969)
produced by Joe Mansano (UK)
A sort of UK equivalent of *Fire Corner*. The flip was first put out on Blue Cat and was re-issued so many times I've lost count.

- *Trial Of Pama Dice / Jughead Returns, Version 1*
Lloyd, Dice And Mum / Nyah Shuffle
Joe JRS 5 (1970)
produced by Joe Mansano (UK)
A rude reggae based on the "Judge Dread" theme which did very well and was later put out again on Sioux.

- *Small Change / Mind Your Business*
Girlie / Girlie And Joe Mansano
Joe JRS 7 (1970)
produced by Joe Mansano (UK)
Girlie could always be relied on to come up with something a bit wide of the mark.

- *Skinhead Revolt / Tony B's Theme*
Joe The Boss / Joe's All Stars
Joe JRS 9 (1970)
produced by Joe Mansano (UK)
Another skinhead classic which Trojan are now making available again for the first time since original release. The flip is an instrumental version of Ray Martell's mournful *She Caught The Train* (JRS 3), later re-issued on Sioux.

- *The Informer / Cool it*
Dice The Boss
Joe JRS 17 (1970)
produced by Joe Mansano (UK)
Still a great track, but the Mansano Sound of 1970 relied on too much of a set formula to guarantee any more than fleeting popularity. The last one on the label.

Jolly

A subsidiary of R & B Discs, this label had just three bonafide JA produced 45s out of its total output of 21 issues. I say bona-fide because most used JA rhythms but had a UK artist like Silver or Richard Selano doing the vocal honours. The JA discs were The Cool Cats' *What Kind Of Man* and *Hold Your Love*, and Phil Pratt's *Sweet Song For My Baby*, of which the latter is a particularly nice slab of rock steady. Most of the others aren't at all bad but personally I prefer the Jamaican originals.

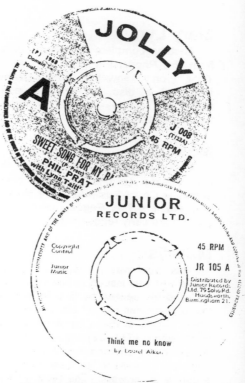

Junior

This was a small independent label based in Handsworth, Birmingham, with around a dozen releases to its name. It was unusual in that some of its releases also appeared on other, more prominent outlets like Ackee (ie Bamboo) and Hillcrest (ie R & B Discs). The Harmonians' *Music Street* and The Schoolboys' *Do It Now* were both put out on Ackee (ACK 107 and 108 respectively) and Junior (JR 112 and 113 respectively). King Cannon's *Reggay Got Soul* also saw issue on Junior (JR103) and Hillcrest (HCT 2).

Others known to be put out on the label were The Movers' *Reggay Rock* and Tony King's *Let Them Talk*. Junior's real rarity though comes in the form of Laurel Aitken's *Think Me No Know* with Reco doing *Trombone Man* on the flip. The label must have received very limited distribution as Junior discs rarely ever turn up on the second hand market. From the few I've heard however, they should certainly not be overlooked if you do come across them. The Aitken offering should be snapped up without fail as it's both very good and, being one of his least-known efforts, very rare.

- **Think Me No Know / Trombone Man**
Laurel Aitken / Reco (but credited to Laurel Aitken on label)
Junior JNR 105 (1969)
produced by Laurel Aitken and Junior Lincoln (UK)
Something a bit different from Laurel here. A good song, but the backing wasn't pure reggae.

London (reggae series)

I thought I'd mention this one briefly as most (if not all) of its output was of JA origin. Many of the sides were leased from the Jamaican Federal label (such as The Gaylettes' *Son Of A Preacher Man*, which also came out on Big Shot) and were by artists such as Jackie Mittoo, Ken Lazirus, Ernie Smith and Eddie Lovette. All four had LPs put out by London. Federal was one of the more commercial-oriented JA studios (which must've suited EMI down to the ground) and, as such, there is little "hard" reggae to be found here.

Mary Lyn

Another complete mystery. Apart from Pat Rhoden's version of *Time Is Tight*, I only know that Denzil Dennis also had a disc out on this label. Significant feature - different coloured labels on either side!

Melody

Possibly put out by Melodisc, the only release on this label I've come across is Count Busty And The Rudies' *You like it / The Reggay* which is a pretty good early reggae outing.

Moodisc

This label was primarily an outlet for productions from JA producer Harry Mudie and was issued in two separate series, the first being put out by Trojan / B & C and the second by R & B Discs after Mudie switched his allegiance. Mudie made particular use of his earliest rhythms and versioned them time and time again. Many of these formative productions can be found on Moodisc's *Mudie's Mood* album (TBL132) which is still available as I write on a JA repressing. The tracks on this LP, and the I Roy DJ cuts from '71, represent the best and most enduring of his work. The second series re-issued some of the earlier sides and in fact lasted until '75 with Dennis Walks (who did the classic *Heart Don't Leap* in '69) as the label's mainstay.

- **Musically Red / Bratah**
Winston Wright & Mudie's All Stars
Moodisc MU 3501 (1970)
produced by Harry Mudie
Nice organ version of Dennis Walks' *Heart Don't Leap*. Also on Moodisc's *Mudie's Mood* compilation.

Nu-Beat / Newbeat

Nu-Beat was Pama's first subsidiary label and has already been covered to some extent in chapter one's leading article on the company. A lot of the earliest and best skinhead reggae is to be found here in the form of Clancy Eccles' *Festival '68*, Alton Ellis' *La La Means I Love You* and *Mini Really Fit Them*, Lloyd Tyrell's (aka Charmers) *Mr Rhya*, and around a dozen storming releases from Laurel Aitken. Nuff said.

For reasons best known to Pama, the label underwent a slight change of title early in '70 and then tended to concentrate on UK recorded material. The good quality Aitken releases continued (at least until he started to go down the road to commercialdom) and there was also a quite startling tune from a new DJ called Tiger (*Souls Of Africa*). Although Tiger promised much, many of his subsequent sides were soppy, sentimental tunes with a spoken lyric. In addition, there was homegrown material from Winston Groov(e)y, The Freedom Singers (UK), The Marvels and Cock And The Woodpeckers which was generally pretty weak when contrasted with the earlier Nu-Beat stuff.

Most of these Newbeat discs are very easy to get hold of these days in nothing short of mint condition, which suggests that they were either poor sellers or that Pama over-estimated their sales potential, pressed too many copies and thus saturated the market. Newbeat shut up shop late in '71, a real case of coming in with a bang and going out with a whimper.

Above: Laurel Aitken, the Godfather Of Ska and High Priest Of Reggae.

- **_Train To Vietnam / Skaville To Rainbow City_**
The Rudies
Nu-Beat NB 001 (July 1968)
produced by Palmer Brothers (UK)
Along the lines of The Pyramids' _Train Tour To Rainbow City_ on President, but miles better. Also on Pama's _Nu-Beat's Greatest Hits_ (ECO 6) and _Rock Steady Cool_ (PMLP 7-SP) compilation albums.

- **_Festival '68 / I Really Love You_**
Clancy Eccles
Nu-Beat NB 006 (1968)
produced by Clancy Eccles
A real frantic effort from Clancy, the pace never lets up on this one.

- **_La La Means I Love You / Give Me Your Love_**
Alton Ellis
Nu-Beat NB 014 (1968)
produced by Duke Reid
 A cover of The Delfonics' slow soul biggie, Alton's classic version was re-pressed again on Newbeat in '71 due to popular demand. On _Nu-Beat's Greatest Hits_ and _Rock Steady Cool_ too.

- **_Rhythm Hips / Deltone Special_**
Ronald Russell / Soul Rhythms
Nu-Beat NB 019 (1968)
produced by Eric Barnet
Out of all the top labels for skinhead reggae, Nu-Beat was definitely one of the very best and most consistent. This was nice suggestive early reggae and was the vocal cut to _The Horse_ on Gas. Also on _Nu-Beat's Greatest Hits_ and _Reggae Hits '69 Volume 1_.

- **_Mini Really Fit Them / Soul Train_**
Alton Ellis And The (Soul) Flames
Nu-Beat NB 020 (December 1968)
produced by Alton Ellis
One of his first self-productions and on which his backing group were much in evidence. Also on _Rock Steady Cool_.

- **_Woppi King / Mr Soul_**
Laurel Aitken
Nu-Beat NB 024 (1969)
produced by Laurel Aitken (UK)
The first in a long run of classic Pama sides from the High Priest Of Reggae. The lyrics deal with re-incarnation and are akin to the sort of thing Prince Buster was putting over in _Ghost Dance_. All interesting stuff. Also on his long-deleted and much sought-after _High Priest Of Reggae_ compilation on Pama (PSP 1012).

- **Hailes Sellasie / Blues Dance**
Laurel Aitken / Laurel Aitken & Girlie
Nu-Beat NB 032 (1969)
produced by Laurel Aitken (UK)
He did a few on the "Sellasie" theme around this time, but this one was popular more for its danceability than the lyrics. Also on *High Priest Of Reggae*.

- **Landlords And Tenants / Everybody Suffering**
Laurel Aitken
Nu-Beat NB 044 (1969)
produced by Laurel Aitken (UK)
This was featured briefly in the dire 1986 flick, *Absolute Beginners*. The subject matter really harked back to the first wave of Jamaican immigrants to arrive in the UK back in the Fifties (when the film was set). Also on *High Priest Of Reggae*.

- **Jesse James / Freedom**
Laurel Aitken
Nu-Beat NB 045 (1969)
produced by Laurel Aitken (UK)
Really good for dancing to, this one. Found its way onto *High Priest Of Reggae* (where it was in partial stereo!) and *This Is Reggae Volume 1*.

- **Pussy Price / Gimme Back Mi Dollar**
Laurel Aitken
Nu-Beat NB 046 (1969)
produced by Laurel Aitken (UK)
The title says it all. On Pama's classic *Birth Control* compilation of rude reggae cuts (SECO 32), now long overdue for release by some enterprising person.

- **Skinhead Train / Kent People**
Laurel Aitken / The Gruvy Beats (but credited to Laurel Aitken)
Nu-Beat NB 047 (1969)
produced by Laurel Aitken (UK)
Another great one on the "train" theme and probably slightly easier to find than the other "skinhead" 45s (if that's possible).

- **Mr Popcorn / Share Your Popcorn**
Laurel Aitken / The Gruvy Beats
Newbeat NB 048 (1970)
produced by Laurel Aitken (UK)
This was inspired by a series of James Brown
US Soul hits (*Mother Popcorn, Let A Man Come In And Do The Popcorn*, etc) and was the first to bear a red and white Newbeat label. It was also on *High Priest Of Reggae* and *Sixteen Dynamic Reggae Hits* (PMP 2015). There must've been a bit of a mix-up at Pama Mission Control since white label copies of *Benwood Dick / Skinhead Invasion* also exist on NB 048.

- *Scandal In A Brixton Market / Soul Grinder*
Laurel Aitken & Girlie
Nu-Beat NB 050 (1970)
produced by Laurel Aitken (UK)
This reverted to the Nu-Beat label and inspired Pama's LP of the same name (ECO 8).

- *Souls Of Africa / Dallas Texas*
Tiger
Newbeat NB 052 (1970)
produced by Laurel Aitken (UK)
Back on course for the Newbeat label this time. This guy never cut another tune as good as this again. Also on Pama's especially rare *Reggae For Days* compilation (ECO 34).

- *Reggae Popcorn / Take Me Back*
Laurel Aitken
Newbeat NB 057 (1970)
produced by Laurel Aitken (UK)
Much slower than his previous sides, this marked the end of a run of around a dozen seminal Aitken 45s on the label.

Pama

Already covered in detail in one, Pama's headline label is perhaps less collectable than its subsidiaries due to the hefty element of American soul it contained leased from minor US labels. Most of these came out on mauve labels with silver writing but had almost completely died out by the end of 1970. Reggae and rock steady releases tended to be put out on orange labels. In fact, out of Pama's total output of 146 issues, around 56 emanated from the other side of the Atlantic or were by The Mohawks, Pama's own soul outfit, who had some measure of success on the continent with *The Champ*. The group did however cash in on the reggae boom later on with *Skinhead Shuffle*.

Of the JA lot, some of the best sides were put out by Clancy Eccles (*C.N Express*), The Termites (the rude *Push It Up*) and Lloyd Tyrell (*Birth Control*, which The Specials later utilised for *Too Much Too Young*). The most consistent stream of reggae issues came after '71 and included a cross-section of JA and UK material.

Pama's compilation LPs, many of which were put out on its budget-priced Economy series, were second to none in the reggae album stakes bar a couple of non-reggae efforts from various choirs, gospel singers, Jamaican humourists and the like. As a starting point, the two *Reggae Hits '69* compilations are suggested as well as the first *This Is Reggae* set. Unfortunately, Pama

REGGAE HOT 15

This Week	Last Week		
1	(4)	WET DREAM	Max Romeo UNITY—503
2	(1)	HOW LONG WILL IT TAKE	Pat Kelly GAS—115
3	(3)	SEND ME SOME LOVING	Derrick Morgan CRAB—23
4	(2)	IF IT DON'T WORK OUT	Pat Kelly GAS—125
5	(7)	BAFF BOOM	The Tennors CRAB—26
6	(5)	MY WHOLE WORLD IS FALLING DOWN	Ken Parker BAMBOO—1
7	(9)	SAVE THE LAST DANCE	Laurel Aitken NU BEAT—039
8	(13)	SOCK IT TO ME SOUL BROTHER	Bill Moss PAMA—765
9	(6)	WHAT AM I TO DO	Tony Scott ESCORT—805
10	(8)	PEYTON PLACE	Donald Lee UNITY—519
11	(10)	MAN ON MOON	Derrick Morgan CRAB—30
12	(15)	WANTED	Baba Dise GAS—118
13	(11)	JUST ONCE IN MY LIFE	Ernest Wilson and Freddy CRAB—21
14	(12)	THROW ME CORN	Winston Shan BULLET—399
15	(14)	SLIP AWAY	Slim Smith UNITY—520

PAMA RECORDS
78 Craven Park Road
London, NW10
Phone:
01-965 2267/8/9

albums are as rare as gold dust these days and, even if you've got a few hundred quid to spend on a decent Pama LP collection, you'll find that having the dosh for them is one thing, but locating them in any sort of condition is another.

- **Say What You're Saying / Tears From My Eyes**
Monty (aka Eric) Morris
Pama PM 721 (1968)
produced by Clancy Eccles
Classic early reggae from the former ska star, and a great song too. Trojan's Clandisc label put it on the *Cynthia Richards And Friends* album, and Pama had it on their *Ready Steady Go - It's Rock Steady* compilation (PMLP SP-3).

- **C.N. Express / You Were Meant For Me**
Clancy Eccles / Lee Perry (but credited to Eccles)
Pama PM 722 (1968)
produced by Clancy Eccles
A chugging DJ version of *Say What You're Saying* and another one on the recurring "train" theme. Also on Pama's *Ready Steady Go - It's Rock Steady* compilation. Lee Perry on the flip is a real bonus.

- **Push It Up / Two Of A Kind**
The Termites / Clancy Eccles And Cynthia Richards
Pama PM 729 (1968)
produced by unknown / Clancy Eccles
Superb rude reggae. Again the name "H Robinson" crops up as producer on this, but I reckon he was the arranger. Also on the rude Pama LP *Bang Bang Lulu* (PMLP-4).

- **Birth Control / Return To Peace (actually Overproof)**
Lloyd Tyrell (aka Lloyd Charmers) / King Cannon (but credited to Val Bennett)
Pama PM 792 (1970)
produced by Lloyd Charmers (UK) / Lynford Anderson
A rude reggae classic also on the *Birth Control* LP. Byron Lee did a version on Trojan (TR 7736), but it wasn't as good.

- **Skinhead Shuffle / Bridgeview (but down as Red Cow on label)**
The Mohawks / Don Drummond (but credited to Reco Rodriguez)
Pama PM 798 (1970)
produced by Graham Hawk (UK) / Lloyd Daley
Although a fairly routine instrumental, as an overtly "skinhead" record it certainly deserves a mention. Unfortunately though, it tends to sell on the title rather than the music.

- *Big Seven / Version*
Charlie Ace And Fay / Charlie Ace & Youth Professionals
Pama PM 853 (1972)
produced by Charlie Ace
One of the last great rude reggae tracks and number one in the reggae charts late in '72. It came in a custom sleeve too.

Pama Supreme

Unconnected with Pama's Supreme label (covered later), Pama Supreme concentrated on Pama's commercial end of the market and was also its main outlet for the company's UK stable of male vocal artists - Owen Gray, Pat Rhoden, D D / Denzil Dennis and Eugene Paul were the main ones. As such, a lot of the sides were reggae covers of pop hits of the time (eg. *Candida*, *Crackling Rosie*, and *I Hear You Knocking*) and weren't really up any skinhead's street. Probably the best release is Derrick Morgan's *John Crow Skank* (on the rhythm of Eric Donaldson's *Cherry Oh Baby*) but, frankly, there are hardly any discs on this label that would merit inclusion in the "Top 300".

Pressure Beat

Pressure Beat was Trojan / B & C's continuation of its Amalgamated outlet for Joe Gibbs' productions, which the company aborted (for whatever reason) towards the end of '70. There were just 15 releases between '70 and '73, and it paled in comparison with its more famous forerunner. There were just a few excellent sides tucked away here, notably The Soul Twins' *Pussy Catch A Fire*, Lord Comic's scorching *Jack Of My Trade* and, later in the series, Dennis Brown's first cut of his late Seventies UK chart hit, *Money In My Pocket*.

- *Pussy Catch A Fire / Follow This Beat*
The Two Soul Brothers (actually The Soul Twins) / The Destroyers
Pressure Beat PB 5506 (1970)
produced by Joe Gibbs
A brilliant rude reggae recently re-issued by Trojan on one of their *Adults Only* volumes. Flip was an instrumental version of The Pioneers' *Catch The Beat*.

- **Jack Of My Trade / United We Stand**
(Sir) Lord Comic / Cynthia Richards (with Clancy Eccles)
Pressure Beat PB 5507 (1970)
produced by Joe Gibbs / Clancy Eccles
A rare outing from early DJ, Comic, who was making a comeback around this time. This one had him riding The Techniques' *You Don't Care* rhythm. The flip is a bit of an oddity as it sounds like a Clancy Eccles production and I'm sure he's in there somewhere.

Prince Buster

At some point during 1970, Melodisc created this subsidiary for the Prince's work, although such was the company's haphazard approach to its cataloging and release schedules that much of his output still appeared on Fab. In fact, some of

the material issued on Fab also came out on the Prince Buster label as well. Discs which only went out on white labels without any indication of artist or title made matters even worse.

The most renowned release on this label is Buster's own *Big Five*, which is still one of the most commonly available 45s on the reggae second hand market (it isn't from 1967 as indicated on the label but three years later). There was plenty of other good stuff from Dennis Alcapone, The Ethiopians, The Heptones and John Holt, but many, like Alcapone's *Kings And Castles* (PB 51) were pressed in such tiny quantities that they're almost impossible to find. On the album side, Buster has spasmodically repressed his late Sixties and early Seventies output on the Prince Buster label, like *John Holt's Greatest Hits* and the three volumes of the all-ska *Original Golden Oldies* sets, and these should be quite easy to pick up.

Punch

One of Pama's foremost skinhead reggae labels, Punch hosted a superb range of material from some of the most noted JA production men of the time (Lee Perry, Alvin Ranglin, Lloyd Daley, Rupie Edwards and one from Coxsone Dodd) and artists like The Upsetters, Bob Marley And The Wailers, Dennis Alcapone and Dave Barker, to name but a few.

The great U Roy had his first UK release in the form of the rarely seen *Scandal* (PH 34), but it is the Perry productions which garner the most interest these days. One of the top skinhead reggae cuts is Count Sticky And The Upsetters' *Dry Acid*, although Perry's production on Pat Satchmo's *Hello Dolly* (PH 9) is best given a miss (as are all Satchmo's releases) as he was reggae's answer to Louis Armstrong. Probably the biggest seller on Punch was The Upsetters' *Clint Eastwood*, which followed hot on the heels of their huge *Return Of Django* at the tail end of '69. Crucial stuff.

- **Too Experienced / Mule Jerk**
Winston Francis / Jackie Mittoo
Punch PH 5 (1969)
produced by Coxsone Dodd
One of the few releases Coxsone had out on Pama. Eddie Lovette did a very commercial version of the song on London's Reggae series, and Owen Gray had one on Trojan (TR 670), but Winston's was far and away the best cut of this very appealing song. Also on volume one of Pama's *Straighten Up* series (PMP 2002).

- **Return Of The Ugly / I've Caught You**
The Upsetters / The Upsetters (With Count Sticky)
Punch PH 18 (1969) .
produced by Lee Perry
Two more dazzling instrumentals from the Upsetting Station, these were also on the *Clint Eastwood* LP.

- **Dry Acid / Selassie**
Count Sticky & The Upsetters / The Reggae Boys
Punch PH 19 (1969)
produced by Lee Perry
An all-time skinhead reggae fave also on *Clint Eastwood*. Hard to find in decent nick though.

- **Prisoner Of Love / Soul Juice**
Dave Barker / The Upsetters
Punch PH 20 (1969)
produced by Lee Perry
There must've been some sort of agreement between Perry and Bunny Lee around this time since they were using each other's rhythm tracks on occasion. This used the backing to Slim Smith's great *Slip Away* (see Unity listing later) which was a Bunny Lee production. Likewise, Bunny used Perry's backing track for Val Bennett's *Spanish Harlem* for Slim's vocal cut and so it went on. *Prisoner Of Love* was in Dave's straight vocal style (he also DJ'd) and was featured on *Clint Eastwood*.

- **Clint Eastwood / Lennox Mood**
The Upsetters / Lennox Brown
Punch PH 21 (1969)
produced by Lee Perry
Said by some to be the first "dub" record (purely an accident in my opinion), this was jerky, esoteric stuff which showed the way Perry was to go on some of his weird and wonderful Seventies records. Another "Western" record, this was in fact worlds away from *Return Of Django* and *Live Injection*, and didn't quite click in the same way that they did. Also on the Pama LP of the same name, *This Is Reggae Volume 1* and *Sixteen Dynamic Reggae Hits*.

- **Ram You Hard / Soul Stew**
The Bleechers / The Mediators
Punch PH 23 (1969)
produced by Lee Perry
More great rude reggae from this consistently good outfit. This one uses the backing track to *Dry Acid* and was on the *Birth Control* LP.

Pyramid

The label that gave us Desmond Dekker's *007*, *Israelites* and *It Mek*, also brought JA producer Leslie Kong to the public eye. Initially begun as a subsidiary of the Doctor Bird Group (Trojan revived it briefly in '73-'74), Pyramid's other top acts were The Maytals and Derrick Morgan (with or without his sister Pauline) who notched up 12 and 17 issues respectively out of the label's first phase output of 71 releases. Desmond meanwhile had 20 issues, including an early version of *It Mek* without the made-for-the-charts backing.

As previously explained in the JJ and Doctor Bird label profiles, JJ labels were also used for Pyramid releases even though they weren't produced by JJ Johnson. In fact, *Israelites* appeared with a JJ label for a time after its initial success. Others also affected by this discrepancy were The Mellotones' *Let's Join Together* (PYR 6060), Derrick Morgan's *What's Your Grouse* and *Johnny Pram Pram* (PYR 6061 and 6063 respectively), The Maytals' *Scare Him* (PYR 6064), and The Pioneers' *Pee Pee Cluck Cluck* (PYR 6065). There were two all Desmond Dekker LPs - *007* and *Israelites* - although the latter was totally eclipsed by Trojan's *This Is Desmond Dekker* LP, which contained most of his significant Pyramid singles.

The second phase of the label contained, as might be expected, the harder reggae sounds of the earlier Seventies from the likes of Gregory Isaacs, Leo Simpson, and The Meditations, and is nowhere near as collectable as the earlier Doctor Bird output. There are however one or two DJ discs in the series by I Roy and Dennis Alcapone which shouldn't necessarily be overlooked. Pyramid was still one of the classic Sixties rock steady and reggae labels that really brought the music mass exposure in the UK. Just think of all those thousands of copies of *Israelites* nestling in people's record collections throughout the land.

- **007 (Shanty Town) / El Torro**
Desmond Dekker & the Aces /
Beverley's All Stars (but actually by
Roland Alphonso)
Pyramid PYR 6004 (1967)
produced by Leslie Kong
One of the first records to break Jamaican music in the UK reaching number 14 in the Top 20 in April 1967. On countless compilation LPs over the years, but originally included on the Pyramid LP of the same name (DLM 5007) and (later) Trojan's *This Is Desmond Dekker* (TTL 4) and *Double Dekker* (TRLD 401).

- **Tougher Than Tough (aka Rudy's In Court) / Song For My Father**
Derrick Morgan / Roland Alphonso
Pyramid PYR 6010 (1967)
produced by Leslie Kong
Another one on the "Judge Dread" theme which also crossed over to the white market in a big way. Also on Derrick's *Best Of* LP on Pyramid (DLMB 5014). He re-cut it again for the Horse label in the mid-Seventies as *Rasta Don't Fear.*

- **Woman A Grumble / Don't Be A Fool**
Derrick Morgan
Pyramid PYR 6039 (1968)
produced by Leslie Kong
Another fine effort from Derrick, the female backing singers seem to be saying "Shit" throughout the record! Also on *Best Of* and *Club Rock Steady '68.* Flip was a non-ska re-issue from the early Island days.

- **Me Naw Give Up / Dreadnaught**
Derrick Morgan / Baba Brooks
Pyramid PYR 6053 (1968)
produced by Leslie Kong
This was almost reggae, but wasn't quite there yet. Also on *Best Of.* There were some excellent ska re-issues on the B sides of some of these Pyramid discs and *Dreadnaught* was originally put out on Black Swan in '64.

- **Do The Reggay / Motoring**
The Maytals / Beverley's All Stars
Pyramid PYR 6057 (1968)
produced by Leslie Kong
It may've been the first record to appear in the UK with the word "Reggay" (sic) in the title, but it was really still rock steady. The band go into a real frenzy on this one, and the heavy bass rhythm bobs and weaves in and out with an electric guitar punctuating the notes. Great stuff. Also on *The Trojan Story Volume 1.*

- **Israelites / The Man**
Desmond Dekker & the Aces / Beverley's All Stars
Pyramid PYR 6058 (1968)
produced by Leslie Kong
This one should need no introduction. The first reggae number one here in the UK, getting there after several months of exposure in the clubs. Also on his *Israelites* LP on Pyramid (DLM 5013) and Trojan's *Reggae Chartbusters Volume 1* in split stereo. *Israelites* was a Top Ten hit all over again in '75 and Des was once more in the public eye.

- **Don't Trouble Trouble / Double Action**
The Maytals / Beverley's All Stars
Pyramid PYR 6066 (1969)
produced by Leslie Kong
Just about the last great record on the label. Loud and jerky and all about botheration. Never put on album at the time.

Opposite page: Desmond Dekker, Hyde Park, 1969 (photo by Barry Plummer)

Q

A very short-lived Trojan / B & C subsidiary, this label dealt solely in productions from one of the earliest sound system operators in the UK, Count Suckle, who ran the Cue (hence the label's name) Club in Paddington's Praed Street. I've only ever found two singles on Q. One was Suckle's own *Please Don't Go / Bread On The Table* with Freddie Notes And The Rudies (Q2201) and the other release was Seventies reggae star Jimmy Lindsay's *Tribute To Jimi Hendrix*, which pretty much speaks for itself. Suckle's *Chicken Scratch* (the Cue Club's in-house dance routine) was put out on Trojan's *Funky Chicken* compilation LP (TBL 137), but as far as I know was never issued on a 45.

Rainbow

Melodisc appeared to use Rainbow as an overspill and stop-gap label after Blue Beat had been dissolved and Fab took over. There were just 12 substantiated releases by UK-based artists such as Laurel Aitken, Sugar Simone and Paula And The Jetliners, and a couple of JA ones by Prince Buster. There isn't much to commend it beyond the Buster output, although Doreen Campbell's *Rude Girls* (with Reco) is okay. Reco (aka Rico), incidentally, ranked alongside the legendary Don Drummond in the trombone stakes (although Don always claimed Reco was better) and was part of Melodisc's in-house backing crew, with UK producer Siggy Jackson often at the controls. Along with Laurel Aitken and Owen Gray, he was an early migrant to the UK, arriving in 1962, and hence appears on a great many UK-produced ska, rock steady and reggae discs.

Randy's

Yet another Trojan / B & C subsidiary specialising in productions from JA producer V Chin and his JA label Impact. The label's most successful artist by far was Jimmy London who had a sizeable reggae hit towards the end of '71 with a version of *Bridge Over Troubled Waters*. There are a few good Ethiopians sounds (*True Man* and *Mr Tom*), one of the best (and later) outings by The Melodians in the form of the glorious *Passion Love*, and two rude reggae goodies from Nora Dean (*Want Man*) and Max Romeo (*Close To Me*). With a tendency towards patchiness, there is really only a handful of the label's output of 36 releases which could be classed as above average.

Reggae

This label was set up by Graeme Goodall, the man behind Doctor Bird and Attack (initially anyway) and the revived Treasure Isle label, and was designed to showcase the talents of UK producers Joe Mansano and Phillip Chen. Not that he got very far, as the label put out just half a dozen or so sides between '69 and '70. Most of what's on offer though is superb, like Mansano's productions on Pama Dice's *Brixton Fight* and *Brixton Pum Pum Wrecker*, and King Horror's *Slave Driver*, which was put out again by Sioux in '72 under the name King Reggie. The Chen productions tend to be much weaker, and his work on The Message (who were also on Trojan's revived Doctor Bird label) isn't too hot. The label folded around the same time as Attack's first phase.

One important point to note is that another label called Reggae surfaced in the mid-Seventies, but had nothing to do with its earlier namesake. The labels for this one were a yellowish colour with a picture of a bee in the top left hand corner, whereas Goodall's effort had light blue colouring and a very plain design.

- *Brixton Fight / Tea House*
Pama Dice / The Opening
Reggae REG 3001 (1970)
produced by Joe Mansano (UK)
Another saga about local sound system clashes. The flip is a nice Upsetters-inspired organ tune. The other really ace tune on this label is called *Brixton Pum Pum Wrecker* (REG 3002), but as I've only got it on a white label pressing, I don't have the necessary details. Mary Whitehouse might raise an eyebrow at it though.

Revolution (rock steady and reggae series)

The origins of the Revolution label are a bit of a mystery, but it was probably initiated by a major, possibly Immediate, and then continued as an independent after Immediate went out of business. Started late in '68, Revolution had three separate series: rock steady, reggae, and pop.

Most of the productions on the rock steady and reggae series were by Dave Hadfield (D & H Productions), and covered mainly home-grown material from Owen Gray, Danny And Cherry, The Carols and The Gladiators (who were almost certainly not the JA outfit who recorded for Studio One). Owen Gray had an entire LP put out on Rock Steady Revolution (*Hits Of '69*) with the label's house band, Maximum Breed, which consisted of covers of the biggest commercial successes reggae had in the late Sixties. This was also issued on the Blue Elephant label on the continent.

For some obscure reason, the label has become very collectable in recent years which has long puzzled me since 95% of its output is, frankly, absolute tosh. Notable feature - its 45s had specially designed company sleeves, which was most unusual for a minor reggae / rock steady label (perhaps the owners had illusions of grandeur). It was very much a cash-in effort on reggae's initial success and died a death around mid-1970. Having said that, another Revolution label appeared around '73 (with a pink label) but, having parted with my one and only disc on it about fifteen years ago, I can't say whether or not it was linked to the earlier set-up. I've never seen another one since.

Rhino

In association with Creole, this was another of EMI's attempts to exploit the reggae market. Rhino was actually fairly successful in that Bruce Ruffin's *Mad About You* did reach the UK Top Ten early in 1973. Most of its output was - you've guessed it - on a very commercial level with Desmond Dekker and Winston Francis (who came to the UK after recording for Coxsone Dodd) featuring prominently. The best sides though are those Dave Barker turned out, notably *Hot Line*, *Smooths 'N' Sorts* (one for Richard Allen fans here) and *Money Is The Poor People's Cry*. Also, if Lee Perry's weirder efforts are up your street, then The Upsetters' *Cloak And Dagger* LP is a good, but very rare, find.

Rio

Rio was the earliest outlet of the Doctor Bird Group and its '62 to '66 releases were primarily in the ska vein. The cream of the crop of its 1967 rock steady sides were collected together nicely on Trojan's *You Left Me Standing* compilation LP (TTL 9), and included The Rulers' *Copasetic*, *Don't Be A Rude Boy* and *Wrong 'Em Boyo*, along with the Young Errol Dunkley's *You're Gonna Need Me* and *Love Me Forever*. There was also some excellent Studio One material issued during the latter part of the label's output from the likes of The Soul Brothers, Derrick Morgan and The Gaylads. The Ethiopians' *Train to Skaville* (a JJ Johnson production) even broke into the UK Top 40 in September '67. The label was superseded by Doctor Bird and its other outlets at the end of that year.

- **Dun Dead Already / Stay In My Lonely Arms**
The Ethiopians / Bob Andy
Rio R 126 (1967)
produced by Coxsone Dodd
There were a lot of good sounds on Rio, but most of them came just prior to '67. This was one of The Ethiopians' best on the label.

- **Train To Skaville / You Are The Girl**
The Ethiopians / The Gladiators (but credited to The Ethiopians)
Rio R 130 (1967)
produced by JJ Johnson
Got into the UK Top 40 and went into the *New Musical Express* Top 30. Another ground-breaking record along with similar chart successes from Desmond Dekker, Prince Buster and The Skatalites in the first half of '67. A very hard bassline makes it particularly distinctive. Also on *The Trojan Story Volume 1* and the group's own mega-rare *Engine 54* LP on WIRL (WIRL 1053).

- **Winey Winey / I Don't Care**
The Kingstonians And The JJ All Stars
Rio R 140 (1967)
produced by JJ Johnson
The group's first UK record, but the last one on Rio, *Winey Winey* was a big success in late '67 and was included on Trojan's *You Left Me Standing* and WIRL's *Club Rock Steady '68* LPs. It was also covered by Byron Lee And The Dragonaires on their Trojan album *Rock Steady Explosion* (TRLS 5).

Rude Boy

Rude Boy was administered briefly by Hala-Gala, a company based in Beckenham in Kent specialising in Guyanese and South American music and films. There was possibly just the one issue, which was partly by a guy called Terry Nelson, who also had non-JA music put out on the main Hala-Gala label, Dice and Blue Beat. Terry 'n' Fraser's *Beng Beng Chitty / Soul Food* was most probably a dreadful cash-in on the '69 reggae boom. One for musical masochists only.

Rymska

Another non-entity, this label was probably put out around '66, but contained nothing in the way of information about dates or productions. The only release that ever turns up these days is Kent Walker And The All Stars', *One Minute To Zero* (RYM 103). This was a good ska number and, in keeping with all the weird and wonderful things that happen with Jamaican music, was also included on volume three of Pama's *This Is Reggae*. Why Pama should put out an obscure ska track on a full-blown reggae LP is totally beyond me, but Rymska might conceivably have been an early Palmer Brothers venture.

Shades

Two non-entities in a row! Shades surfaced around '71 and specialised in productions from Ian Smith on his group The Inner Mind (mentioned earlier in this book). Only a couple of sides were ever put out, including one called *Jesse James Rides Again* which I've never heard. A very difficult one to find.

Sioux

Sioux was a subsidiary of Ed Kassner's President label which had already dabbled briefly in Jamaican music between '67 and '70 with releases from the Four Gees, The Pyramids, The Hammers (who also appeared on Pama's Gas subsidiary) and Little Grants And Eddie (Grant). Grant was of course a member of the chartbusting Equals outfit and, as a native West Indian, probably influenced Kassner sufficiently to try his luck with the Jamaican sound. The Pyramids made some impact on the UK charts with their *Train Tour To Rainbow City* (based largely on Prince Buster's *Train To Girls Town*) and also cropped up on President's Jay Boy subsidiary under such aliases as the E.K. (Ed Kassner) Bunch, The Bedbugs, The Rough Riders and The Alterations. They later metamorphosised into Symarip.

Which basically brings us to why Sioux was set up. The Equals were really President's bread and butter and, after their glory days finished in the early Seventies, the label was going through a very lean period. Kassner was therefore looking eagerly for renewed success from other sources to keep his label afloat. A few of Sioux's releases actually came from JA producer Harry J under his Roosevelt banner and included Joe Higgs' *The World Is Spinning Around* and *Wave Of War*. A fair amount were just re-issues from other labels and included some of Joe Mansano's material, thereby providing another way of picking up some of the Joe label's output.

Other notables were Phyllis Dillon's *In The Ghetto*, Exodus' *Pharoah's Walk* (a re-issue from the Duke label), and Lloyd The Matador's DJ version of the Ethiopians' rock steady classic, *Engine 54*. Sioux has the distinction of being one of the few early Seventies reggae labels which is still very easy to find today. Its four compilation LPs (*King Of The Road*, *Swan Lake*, *Unchained* and *With These Hands*) are on the other hand almost impossible to locate.

Ska Beat

Ska Beat actually followed on from the R & B label around the end of '64 and used the same catalogue numbers and prefix. This revamped effort rivalled Doctor Bird and Island in the ska stakes with a series of superb sides from Roland

Alphonso, Lord Tanamo, who did *I'm In The Mood For Ska (Love)*, The Wailers, Derrick Morgan and Baba Brooks. Like both these labels, Ska Beat covered the whole gamut of Jamaican producers such as Coxsone Dodd, Duke Reid and Derrick Harriott with several sides from their respective stables appearing consecutively in short spurts of up to seven releases at a time.

The label never really got going on the rock steady front however as just 13 issues appeared during '67, the most famous of which was Dandy's *Rudy, A Message To You*. The label folded some time that year (the title was already out of date of course) and R & B Discs then used its Giant, Jolly and Caltone outlets instead. R & B never again had a label which provided such a wide coverage of the most noted JA producers of the time. Overall, a very collectable label which unfortunately largely misses out on the "Top 300" since most of its releases fall outside the time span covered.

- **Rudy, A Message To You / Till Death Us Do Part**
Dandy And His Group
Ska Beat JB 273 (1967)
produced by Dandy (UK)
A British record on the "Rude Boy" theme that was on a par with all the similar stuff coming out of JA. Such a good song that The Specials revived it for a UK Top Tenner in 1980. Reco played on the Two Tone version and the original. Also re-pressed on the Jolly label in '68 after Ska Beat had been discontinued, and later put on *The Trojan Story Volume 1*.

Smash

Another of Trojan / B & C's subsidiaries, this one dabbled in productions from Bunny Lee, Keith Hudson (who was a newcomer to the scene then) and Clancy Collins, but never settled into any definite pattern. One of the most notable releases was Dennis Alcapone's *Ball Of Confusion* which was put out under his own name of Dennis Smith and was one of his very earliest sides. But despite a few decent issues, Smash certainly wasn't in Trojan's premier league.

- **Wake The Nation / One Hundred Tons Of Version**

U Roy & Jeff Barnes / Jeff Barnes

Smash SMA 2311 (1970)

produced by Bunny Lee

One of the few records Roy did for Bunny Lee, this was somewhat overshadowed by his Duke Reid sides. *Wake The Nation* rides Lester Sterling's *Reggae In The Wind* (GAS 103), but the DJ is way down in the mix unfortunately. Nice DJ cut of Slim's *Everybody Needs Love* on the flip.

- **Hard Life / Version**

Marlene Webber / Collins' All Stars

Smash SMA 2322 (1971)

produced by Clancy Collins

Marlene sings about the limited opportunities open to her to make ends meet. Very heavy rhythm which could've been laid in JA. On *Tighten Up Volume 4*, but surprisingly difficult to find on 45.

Song Bird

Contrary to what many people think, Trojan never initially designated Song Bird as an exclusive subsidary for Derrick Harriott's productions. There were a few from Stranger Cole, Lloyd Charmers and Winston Lowe in the formative stages of the label. Harriott took over the reins with The Kingstonians' *The Clip* (SB 1011) and continued with a quite startling series of sides from his session band The Crystalites. These included a series of Spaghetti Western influenced discs like *Overtaker*, *Undertaker*, *Undertaker's Burial*, *The Bad* and *True Grit* (with percussionists Bongo Herman and Les Chen). Most of these were collected together nicely on Trojan's *Undertaker* compilation LP of Harriott material (TBL 114).

The label made real headway in 1970 with The Kingstonians' *Singer Man*, Harriott's own cover of The Temptations' *Message From A Blackman*, and The Crystalites' *Psychedelic Train* (with the Chosen Few). However, after a number of hard-hitting Ethiopians sides (such as *No Baptism* and *Good Ambition*), and some good DJ material from Scotty (*Sesame Street* and *Riddle I This*), Song Bird seemed to move towards a more commercial direction. Having said that, most of the 170 sides contain some excellent skinhead reggae and are well worth picking up.

- **Long About Now / Come See About Me**

Bruce Ruffin & The Temptations

Song Bird SB 1002 (1969)

produced by Lloyd Charmers

Very much in the style of Pat Kelly and The Uniques - soulful and mellow. A little-known and under-rated classic. And no, they definitely weren't Motown's Temptations.

- **_In The Spirit / Duckey Luckey_**
Lloyd Charmers
Song Bird SB 1007 (1969)
produced by Winston Lowe
In The Spirit was actually the B side (the top-side was very so-so). A tried and tested Charmers' tune now re-issued by Trojan on their new _Skinhead Revolt_ CD compilation.

- **_The Undertaker / Stop That Man_**
The Crystalites
Song Bird SB 1017 (1970)
produced by Derrick Harriott
These Crystalites' Spaghetti Western tunes were very popular with skinheads, and so much so that there were loads of the buggers! Also on Trojan's _The Undertaker_ LP. Nice instrumental cut of Keith And Tex's _Stop That Train_ on the flip.

- **_Singer Man / Version_**
The Kingstonians / The Crystalites
Song Bird SB 1019 (1970)
produced by Derrick Harriott
One of the biggest reggae sellers of the year, it typiified The Kingstonians' ethnic vocals . Also on _Tighten Up Volume 3_, _Reggae Reggae Reggae_ and their Trojan LP of the same name (TBL 113).

- **_Good Ambition / Version_**
The Ethiopians / The Crystalites
Song Bird SB 1047 (1970)
produced by Derrick Harriott
Very catchy number also on _Tighten Up Volume 4_.

Sound Of Jamaica
A solitary Sound Of Jamaica release appeared as part of Clancy Collins' Down Beat label in '68. Lord Charles And His Band's _Jamaican Bits And Pieces / Ja Island Sound_ (CR 0014/JAI) was calypso fused with rock steady and is actually quite listenable.

Sound System
Reputedly issued by R & B Discs, this obscure label spawned just five releases from the likes of Glen Adams (but credited to Glade Soul) and Neville Hinds. A very difficult one to track down.

Spinning Wheel
Of all Trojan / B & C's subsidiaries, Spinning Wheel releases are among the hardest to find. From only ten issues, Stranger Cole's _Crying Every Night_ (also put out on Camel) was its only seller.

There were a couple of UK productions on The Rudies and The Cimmarons as well as some mega-rare Upsetters sides which were produced by Melanie Jonas rather than Lee Perry. Expect to pay around a tenner for these.

Spur

A subsidiary of Creole Records, Spur put out just three singles in '71-'72 by Delroy Wilson, Alton Ellis and JA producer and recording artist Keith Hudson. Hudson produced all the Spur sides and they reflected the harder, more ethnic sounds of the early Seventies. Not easy to find.

Star

Possibly put out by Melodisc, the only Star release I've located to date is Sir Washington's *Apollo 11 / When I Kiss You* (ST 1). This UK-recorded effort was very much a cash-in on the topical '69 moon landing and was in a slightly similar vein to SS Binns' *Boss A Moon* which came out on Escort.

Studio One

Much of the Coxsone profile earlier in this chapter mirrors the Studio One label since many artists appeared on both outlets and Studio One was, in effect, Coxsone's sister label. A wholly Coxsone Dodd produced effort, Studio One put out material by The Heptones, Alton Ellis, Ken Boothe, Jackie Mittoo And The Soul Vendors (who later became Sound Dimension). Studio One releases are generally harder to find than Coxsone ones, but The Heptones' *Fat Girl* (credited to Ken Boothe on the label as *Fatty Fatty*) and Boothe's cover of the Eurovision success *Puppet On A String* are by far the most common. So, like Coxsone, there are a few Studio One sides that were particularly big sellers and turn up time and time again. Album-wise, we're talking gold dust - copies of The Heptones' first and second albums on the label can easily fetch in the region of £100 these days.

- **See Them A Come / Have A Good Time**
Mr Foundation (actually Zoot Simms) / Ken Parker
Studio One SO 2001 (1967)
produced by Coxsone Dodd
Another personal favourite. Also on Island's *Put It On - It's Rock Steady*.

122

- *Fatty Fatty (actually titled Fat Girl) / Mother Word*
The Heptones / Delroy Wilson (but both sides actually credited to Ken Boothe)
Studio One SO 2014 (1967)
produced by Coxsone Dodd
One of the biggest sellers on the label and later covered in fine style by Lloydie (Charmers) And The Lowbites on their *Censored* LP (Lowbite LOW 001). Included on The Heptones' first album on Studio One (SOL 9002) and (later) Bamboo's first volume of the *Natural Reggae* series (BLP 201).

- *Put It On / Chinese Chicken*
Jackie Mittoo / Soul Vendors
Studio One SO 2043 (1968)
produced by Coxsone Dodd
One of his few vocal discs. On *Club Rock Steady '68*.

- *Nanny Goat / Smell You Crap (actually Wepp)*
Larry And Alvin / The Jamaican Actions
Studio One SO 2065 (1968)
produced by Coxsone Dodd
According to Dodd, this was the first bona fide reggae record. Later versioned for Sound Dimension's *More Scorcha* on Coxsone, and Dennis Alcapone's *Nanny Version* on Banana.

- *Hello Carol / More Reggae*
The Gladiators / Richard Ace
Studio One SO 2072 (February 1969)
produced by Coxsone Dodd
Fast and echo-laden, this was on Studio One's *Party Time In Jamaica* compilation (SOL 9009).

- *I Shall Be Released / Love Me Always*
The Heptones
Studio One SO 2083 (May 1969)
produced by Coxsone Dodd
Great cover of a Bob Dylan (who?) song re-issued on Bamboo (BAM 11) shortly after Studio One was superseded by the label. Also on the *A Scorcha From Bamboo* compilation of Studio One label cuts (BDLP 202).

Success
A Pama subsidiary devoted entirely to Rupie Edwards' productions, there were a few goodies put out here over just 14 issues. Among them were Rupie's *Promoter's Grouse*, which utilised his excellent *Grandfather Clock* rhythm, and one of John Holt's rare rude reggae outings with *Fat Girl, Sexy Girl*. After Success folded, the producer had another exclusive outlet courtesy of Trojan's Big subsidiary.

* **Promoter's Grouse / Grandfather Clock (actually Go Deh)**
Rupie And Sidy / Cannonball King (but both sides credited to Rupie Edwards All Stars)
Success RE 902 (1969)
produced by Rupie Edwards
Great "studio chatter" version of Winston Wright's *Grandfather Clock*.

* **Fat Girl, Sexy Girl / Man And Woman**
John Holt
Success RE 903 (1970)
produced by Rupie Edwards
One of the very few bawdy records ever made by the usually respectable John.

Sugar

A short-lived off-shoot of Decca, Sugar put out just a couple of commercial reggae 45s and one LP. Best given a miss.

Summit

A subsidiary of Trojan / B & C, Summit dealt exclusively with productions from Leslie Kong, at least until his death in 1971. The bulk of the releases were by The Maytals, The Melodians, Ken Boothe, and The Pioneers, but the label's tendency towards commercialdom has resulted in it largely being ignored by collectors. Generally, only The Maytals' sides (particularly *Peeping Tom* and *Monkey Girl*) are eagerly sought after.

The only two really "hard" cuts are Glen Brown's *Collie And Wine* (SUM 8502) and Samuel The First's *Sounds Of Babylon*, which was a DJ version of The Melodians' legendary *Rivers of Babylon* (SUM 8508). The latter was Summit's biggest seller and reputedly sold well in excess of 50,000 copies when originally issued in the fall of 1970. However, because the bulk of the sales were via the many small specialist outlets who were never included in the British Market Research Bureau's (B.M.R.B) trawl for sales returns, the disc never got the chart placing it was entitled to. It wasn't the only one either as plenty of other reggae waxings also fell into this category.

Opposite page: Toots Hibbert of Toots & The Maytals' fame (photo by Barry Plummer)

After Kong's posthumous material dried up around '72, the label seemed to lose direction and was discontinued by Trojan in '73. Not a classic reggae label, but definitely one with a fair amount of undervalued music well worth a second look.

- *Peeping Tom / Version*
The Maytals / Beverley's All Stars
Summit SUM 8510 (1970)
produced by Leslie Kong
Another of The Maytals' rousing tunes also to be found on their *Monkey Man* LP on Trojan (TBL 107).

- *Monkey Girl / Version*
The Maytals / Beverley's All Stars
Summit SUM 8513 (1971)
produced by Leslie Kong
Never repeated the success of Monkey Man, but still good.

Supreme

Pama seemed to be in a complete dilemma over this one since the first release on both Supreme and Pama Supreme was Junior Byles' *Demonstration* (actually credited on the label as *What The World Is Coming To*). One of Lee Perry's few commercially-biased productions, both releases came out with the same catalogue number (PS 297).

After this false start, Supreme began to develop an identity of its own with a few Coxsone Dodd productions, most notably by Jackie Bernard and The Kingstonians (where they masqueraded under the ridiculous psuedonym of Jack And The Beanstalks), Sound Dimension and Lloyd Robinson (but credited to Mr

Foundation). Otherwise, there were a few mediocre sides from Owen Gray and The Mohawks.

Other notables were The Ethiopians' *Love Bug* / Sound Of Our Forefathers (which also came out on GG) and Dave Barker's straight vocal cut of *Johnny Dollar*, another version of which was produced by Coxsone Dodd and put out on Ackee. Supreme also issued Marley's *I Like It Like This* (SUP 216), which was an early version of his late Seventies biggie *Satisfy My Soul*. At around thirty to forty quid a throw for a decent copy these days, it's also one of the most expensive reggae singles of all time.

- *Time To Pray / Young Budd*
Lloyd Robinson / The Ethiopians (but both sides credited to "Mr Foundation")
Supreme SUP 201 (April 1970)
produced by Coxsone Dodd
A reggae-fied version of The Mellow Larks' number from the early days of the Blue Beat label.

- *Work It Up / Chatty Chatty*
Jack And The Beanstalks (actually the Kingstonians)
Supreme SUP 203 (1969)
produced by Coxsone Dodd
What a way to throw a collector off the scent of two good Coxsone productions? Don't pass this one over in future.

Techniques

This was a Trojan / B & C subsidiary specialising in productions from Winston Riley, who was originally a lead vocalist with The Techniques (hence the label's

name) after Pat Kelly and Bruce Ruffin had done their respective stints. The label is best known for Dave (Barker) And Ansell Collins' chart-topping *Double Barrel* and its follow-up *Monkey Spanner*. Others worth lending an ear to are Winston Wright's organ instrumental *Top Secret*, and two excellent DJ cuts in the form of Prince Jazzbo's *Mr Harry Skank* and Lloyd Young's *High Explosion*. Apart from the Dave And Ansell Collins' sides however, Techniques was never really a source of skinhead reggae. Another point of note is that one of Trojan's rarest LPs, *Who You Gonna Run To* (TBL 134), was put out on Techniques. Try finding this one!

- *Double Barrel / Version*
Dave (Barker) & Ansel Collins / Ansel Collins
Techniques TE 901 (September 1970)
produced by Winston Riley
The second reggae number one and also, like *Israelites*, a hit in America. Included on Trojan's Techniques' LP of the same name (TBL 162), *Club Reggae Volume 1* and *Reggae Chartbusters Volume 3* (TBL 169).

- *Monkey Spanner / Version*
Dave And Ansel Collins
Techniques TE 914 (June 1971)
produced by Winston Riley
Their follow up to *Double Barrel* which also went Top Ten. On *Reggae Chartbusters Volume 3*.

Torpedo

Already mentioned in the Lambert Briscoe article in the UK producers' section in one, Torpedo was set up by The Equals' bassist, Eddie Grant, and UK producer and sound system operator, Lambert Briscoe, during 1970. It's best remembered these days for its Hot Rod All Stars sides and just one or two others. Larry Lawrence twiddled the knobs on a few tracks, notably Errol English's cover of The Small Faces' *Sha La La La Lee*. The B side of this was entitled *A.G.G.R.O.* by an outfit calling themselves The Bovver Boys and, despite the skinhead-flavoured title, it is best avoided.

SKINHEADS DON'T FEAR
(L. Foster)
THE HOT ROD ALL-STARS

The label folded the same year it started, but Grant revived it again in '75. One notable disc in this second series was the unusual re-issue of Baba Brooks' ska classic *One Eyed Giant*, which was originally put out twice on Ska Beat (JB 220 and JB268). Like Sioux, Torpedo label material is still very common these days, although supplies of the Hot Rod All Stars' skinhead sides have all but dried up.

- ***Pussy Got Nine Life / Lick It Back (Boss Sound)***
Hot Rod All Stars
Torpedo TOR 1 (1970)
produced by Lambert Briscoe (UK)
One of their best.

- ***Skinheads Don't Fear / Ten Commandments From The Devil***
Hot Rod All Stars
Torpedo TOR 5 (1970)
produced by Lambert Briscoe (UK)
Another one I've not heard and now very rare due to over-subscribed demand.

- ***Run Like A Thief / Nobody's Fool***
Les Foster
Torpedo TOR 7 (1970)
produced by Les Foster (UK)
Along with *It's Not Impossible* on Joe (DU 53), this was definitely his best-ever reggae record. A UK tune nearly as hard as a JA one.

- ***Moonhop In London / Skinhead Moondust***
Hot Rod All Stars
Torpedo TOR 10 (1970)
produced by Lambert Briscoe (UK)
Two great sides here. *Moonhop In London* is totally different from Derrick Morgan's *Moon Hop*.

Treasure Isle

Originally started by Island as an exclusive outlet for Duke Reid productions, this was the UK counterpart of the Duke's Jamaican Treasure Isle label. Beginning with The Techniques' seminal *You Don't Care* (with Pat Kelly on lead vocals), the label put out a series of classic rock steady sides from the great JA harmony groups of the era - The Melodians, The Paragons (with John Holt), The Silvertones, The Jamaicans, The Three Tops, The Conquerors, and Alton Ellis And The Flames for example. Out of an initial 43 issues, there was hardly a duff track released. Suffice to say that, if rock steady is your particular bag, you can't go wrong with Treasure Isle's '67 and '68 output.

It seemed odd then that Island wrapped up the label during '68. Island were also issuing the Duke's material on their fledgling Trojan outlet (with the occasional duplication) and may have decided that Trojan should subsume his work in future. Trojan was in fact "related" to the Duke anyway in that he was originally known as "The Trojan" (after the name of the van he transported his equipment in), and his first 78 rpm sides were put out on a Trojan label back in the mid-Fifties. Add to this the fact that the earliest of Island's Trojan label singles (ie those in the initial batch of 11) usually carried the banner "A Duke Reid Production" underneath the Trojan emblem, and the theory is probably borne out.

Both Island and Trojan / B & C were quick to exploit the Duke's excellent material with a series of classic compilation LPs. Among these were Island's own *Duke Reid Rocks Steady* (ILP 958), and Trojan's *Soul Of Jamaica* (TRL 3), *Here Comes The Duke* (TRL 6) and *Duke Reid's Golden Hits* (TTL 8). That both companies should give the man and his artists such a high profile is testimony to the quality of the golden sounds of the Treasure Isle studios.

What happened after this is a bit disjointed. Graeme Goodall, the man responsible for the Doctor Bird Group of labels, briefly revived Treasure Isle late in 1969 to supplement his Philligree stable productions on Doctor Bird and Attack. These few releases were primarily devoted to Symarip (*Skinhead Moonstomp*, *La Bella Jig* and *Parson's Corner*), but also included Andy Capp's classic early DJ venture *Pop A Top* (produced by Lynford Anderson), Boris Gardner's *Hooked On A Feeling* (produced by Junior Chung), and a rare white label only issue from Girlie doing a thing called *Boss Cocky* (TI 7053).

The label was again revived by Trojan / B & C in '71 as an exclusive outlet for Reid's productions. This was a pretty curious move by the company given that by that time another outlet existed for his music (Duke Reid). But as you'll no doubt have already gathered from this book, such occurences are by no means uncommon in Jamaican music. This further revived label put out a good deal of

DJ music from Dennis Alcapone and U Roy toasting over tried and tested Treasure Isle rhythms, along with a fair amount of new material from the Duke. Count among those Phyllis Dillon's *One Life To Live, One Love To Give* and *Midnight Confession,* The Ethiopians' *Pirate,* and Justin Hinds' *Mighty Redeemer.*

The label ended on a high note in '73 with Alcapone's *Wake Up Jamaica* (a toast over Joya Landis' biggie from early '69, *Moonlight Lover*), which went to number one in the UK reggae best sellers. Trojan / B & C wound up Treasure Isle at about the same time as the Duke Reid label, largely as a result of the company's slimming-down operation that year, but also because the Duke's ill health had curtailed his production career.

- ### *You Don't Care / Travelling On Bond Street*
The Techniques / Tommy McCook & The Supersonics
Treasure Isle TI 7001 (1967)
produced by Duke Reid
Classic tune here, the rhythm and song were used, covered (even by different producers) and versioned at least a dozen times. A few examples - *Midnight Special* by Jackie Mittoo on Coxsone; *Barbwire* by Nora Dean on Trojan; *Buttercup* by Winston Scotland on Punch; *Meshwire* by Winston Wright on Trojan; and a 1972 re-make of it by Lloyd Sparks (Parks) on Big Shot. The original was on *Duke Reid's Golden Hits* (TTL 8) and *Duke Reid Rocks Steady* (ILP 958).

- ### *Here I Stand / No Good Rudy*
Justin Hinds & The Dominoes
Treasure Isle TI 7002 (1967)
produced by Duke Reid
Great song very much in the late-ska style which was re-done recently in ragga mode. Also on *Duke Reid's Golden Hits.*

- ### *Rock Steady / Wall Street Shuffle*
Alton Ellis And The Flames / Tommy McCook & The Supersonics
Treasure Isle TI 7004 (1967)
produced by Duke Reid
Compare this with *Here I Stand* to see how the beat was slowing down into rock steady. To a large extent, *Rock Steady* was the disc that really kicked the whole rock steady style (and the dance that accompanied it) into play. On *Duke Reid's Golden Hits, Duke Reid Rocks Steady* and *The Trojan Story Volume 1.* Errol Dunkley plagiarised it reggae style around '73-'74 as *Shelly Reggae Rock* for the Count Shelly label.

- ### *Ba-Ba Boom (Festival Song '67) / Real Cool*
The Jamaicans / Tommy McCook & The Supersonics
Treasure Isle TI 7012 (1967)
produced by Duke Reid
Great rippling bass on this one. Also on *Duke Reid's Golden Hits* and the super-rare *Greatest Jamaican Beat* LP on Treasure Isle (DLM 5009), which was re-issued briefly several years back.

- ### *The Same Song / Soul Serenade*
The Paragons / Tommy McCook & The Supersonics
Treasure Isle TI 7013 (1967)
produced by Duke Reid
John Holt on lead vocals here. Great bassline.

Above: Alton Ellis (photo by Vincent St. Hilaire)

- *Once A Man / Persian Cat (aka Persian Ska)*
Justin Hinds & the Dominoes / Tommy McCook & The Supersonics
Treasure Isle TI 7017 (1967)
produced by Duke Reid
Both sides of this were popular. The flip was a Middle Eastern flavoured instrumental featured on *Duke Reid Golden Hits*. *Once A Man* was a first-rate rock steady vocal, later re-cut in reggae by Billy Jack for Trojan's *Queen Of The World* LP.

- *Midnight Hour / Soul For Sale*
The Silvertones / Winston Wright & Tommy McCook
Treasure Isle TI 7027 (1968)
produced by Duke Reid
Great version of Wilson Pickett's classic. On *Duke Reid's Golden Hits*.

- *Skinhead Moonstomp / Must Catch A Train*
Symarip
Treasure Isle TI 7050 (November 1969)
produced by Graeme Goodall for Philligree Productions (UK)
Did someone say predictable? Surely not! Okay then, so this is just about the most well-known made-for-the-skinhead-cult disc ever made, based as it was on Derrick Morgan's *Moon Hop*. But in the sales and popularity stakes, it's certainly lasted the distance and is as popular now as it was on first release and second time around during the Two Tone era in 1980. For anyone who's ever seen it, *Skinhead Moonstomp* was featured briefly in Horace Ove's 1970, film *Reggae*. It was also the title track of Symarip's album of the same name on Trojan (TBL 102) which, although it had an ace sleeve depicting original skins, often left rather a lot to be desired musically. I can't knock it too much though since it's still one of Trojan's most consistent sellers (although the original copy is the most revered). Also on *Reggae Chartbusters Volume 1*.

- *Pop A Top / The Lion Speaks*
Andy Capp (Lynford Anderson) / Reco
Treasure Isle TI 7052 (November 1969)
produced by Lynford Anderson
This was the first and most successful in a brief series of similar *Pop A Top* records which included Fitzroy (Sterling) and Harry (Young)'s *Pop A Top Train* on Escort (ERT 827), Derrick Morgan's *Derrick Top-The-Pop* on Unity (UN 540) and Capp's later *Poppy Show* on Duke (DU 71), all of which were on a jerky, stop-start sort of rhythm.

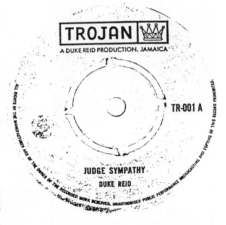

Trojan

As a record company, Trojan is still unrivalled in its success in bringing the music of Jamaica, together with its producers and artists, to the attention of British record buyers. The statistics speak for themselves - in excess of 2,000 singles were put out on the main Trojan label and all its various subsidiaries during a seven year period; as many as 40 subsidiary labels were owned and / or distributed by the company at one particular time; around 250 LPs were issued up until 1975; and the work of some 60-odd producers from both the UK and JA were showcased during its peak period. To attempt to gauge the number of artists who were similarly featured on Trojan labels over the years would be a mammoth task.

I have already covered the rise, fall and rise again of Trojan to a large extent in chapter one, but a brief word on Trojan label releases (ie not the subsidiaries, which are covered elsewhere in this chapter) might be helpful. Island's first run of 11 Trojan singles was put out between July '67 and January '68. The famous "600 series" of Trojan 45s was started around the summer of '68 when Trojan / B & C took up the reins from Island. The earliest discs in this series, which carry all-orange labels and a boxed crown logo, are generally the most sought-after Trojan singles by skinheads.

Included here were the Brother Dan All Stars (*Donkey Returns* and *Read Up*), Alton Ellis (*Breaking Up*), Joya Landis (*Angel Of The Morning*, *Kansas City* and *Moonlight Lover*), tenor saxophonist Val Bennett (*Spanish Harlem*), The Race Fans (*Time Marches On*), The Beltones (*No More Heartaches*) and Denzil Dennis (*Me Nah Worry* and *Donkey Train*). The label's *Tighten Up Volume One* put out in the early months of '69 contained an excellent sample of the biggest hits of the early part of the 600s and is crucial listening for any self respecting skinhead or fan of rock steady and early reggae.

Much of the material was also produced by some of the best JA and UK producers including Duke Reid, Byron Lee, Bunny Lee, Dandy, Harry Johnson, Lynford Anderson, Lee Perry, and Winston Lowe. The latter four were very much part of the "new breed" of Jamaican producers and show how the supremacy of longer standing producers like Duke Reid and Coxsone Dodd was being challenged by '68.

The all-orange label changed to the more familiar orange and white one in mid-'69, although copies of The Pioneers' UK hit, *Long Shot Kick The Bucket*, issued a few months later have surfaced with the former label design. From this point on, a large amount of Leslie Kong material began to appear, notably by the likes of The Maytals (*Monkey Man*, *Pressure Drop* and *Water Melon*), The Melodians (*Sweet Sensation* and *Say Darling Say*), The Pioneers (the aforementioned *Long Shot Kick The Bucket*, *Poor Rameses* and *Samfie Man*), and The Gaylads (*God Loves You Soul Sister* and *There's A Fire*). In fact, Duke Reid, who had hitherto been one of the top producers on the 600 series in terms of releases, was shortly to be largely usurped by Kong's bouncy chartbound reggae of late '69 and '70.

133

Further volumes of the company's *Tighten Up* LP series continued to be enormously successful, as were plenty of superb compilation albums showcasing the individual production talents of (among others) Kong, Reid, Perry, Clancy Eccles, Derrick Harriott and Byron Lee. There were also individual artist packages from The Kingstonians, Freddie Notes And The Rudies, The Ethiopians, The Maytals, The Uniques and many more. Trojan capitalised on the success of the *Tighten Up* series with three volumes of *Reggae Chartbusters*, five of *Club Reggae* and three apiece of *Music House* (named after Trojan's headquarters in Neasden Lane) and *Reggae Jamaica*.

The early Seventies saw the arrival of the company's TRLS LP series, which concentrated on near full-price stereo albums. These tended to be much better quality pressings than the more budget-oriented TTL and TBL series efforts and, in some cases, sported more imaginative sleeves and comprehensive liner notes. The first triple album (volume one of *The Trojan Story*) was put out at the end of '71, a pretty classy package by Trojan's standards. But Trojan's days as kingpin manufacturer of reggae LPs was drawing to a close by late '73 as the quality and quantity of the company's material began to dry up.

Unlike the company's albums, it is probably true to say that only those Trojan label 45s put out between '67 and '70 are eagerly collected these days. In the early 1970s, singles on the label tended to be of an increasingly commercial nature, reflecting the big UK chart hits the main Trojan label was getting at the time - Bob and Marcia's *Pied Piper*, Greyhound's *Black And White* and *Moon River*, The Pioneers' *Let Your Yeah Be Yeah*, and Bruce Ruffin's *Rain* were all very successful during 1971.

Although most of the real ethnic material was put out on 45 via the company's subsidiaries, Trojan label LPs still generally reflected the harder side of reggae right up until '75 - The Silvertones' *Silver Bullets*, Scotty's *School Days*, Dennis Brown's *Super Reggae And Soul Hits*, I Roy's *Many Moods Of I Roy*, and volumes of the *Version To Version* and *Version Galore* DJ compilations are just a few examples of this. The albums also maintained the old orange and white label, whereas the 45s were redesigned circa mid-'71 with a rather bland brown one.

So there you have it. Just to re-iterate, this brief profile has merely covered the material issued on the main Trojan label itself. As the most successful company ever to specialise in Jamaican music, Trojan and its multitude of subsidiary labels justifiably form a large part of this book.

- ### *It's Raining / Sound Of Music*
The Three Tops
Trojan TR 003 (August 1967)
produced by Duke Reid
An early Trojan stormer featured on *The Trojan Story Volume 1* and *Duke Reid Rocks Steady*.

- ### *Love Is A Treasure / Zazuka*
Freddy McKay / Tommy McCook & The Supersonics
Trojan TR 010 (January 1968)
produced by Duke Reid
One of his first discs, this was put out again on Duke in '73 as the flip to DJ Lizzy's cut of it (DU 161).

- **_Donkey Returns / Tribute To Sir K.B_**
Brother Dan All Stars
Trojan TR 601 (July 1968)
produced by Dandy (UK)
Great harmonica (almost) instrumental which was heavily influenced by The Tennors _Let Go Ya Donkey_ on Fab. Also on _Tighten Up Volume 1_ and their _Follow That Donkey_ (TRL 1) LP set.

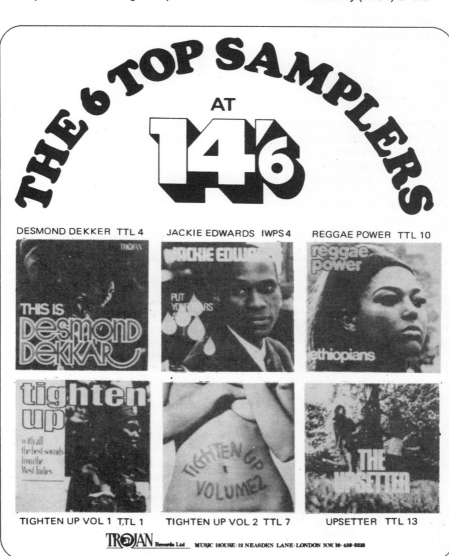

● *Tighten Up / Good Ambition*
The Untouchables (actually Jimmy London & The Inspirations) / Roy Shirley
Trojan TR 613 (1968)
produced by Lee Perry / Bunny Lee
This gave the album series its name and was logically included as the first track on *Tighten Up Volume 1*. Flipside was a reissue from Island's later stages (WI 3125).

● *Me Nah Worry / Hush Don't You Cry*
Denzil Dennis
Trojan TR 615 (November 1968)
produced by Dandy (UK)
Very poppy but without any of the commercial trappings used a few years later. A song along the lines of Lee Perry's *People Funny Boy*, Dandy also used the rhythm for his *The Toast* (TR 618). Denzil apparently also went under the name of D D Dennis.

● *Place In The Sun / Handi-Cap*
David Isaacs / The Upsetters
Trojan TR 616 (1968)
produced by Lee Perry
Superb cover of Stevie Wonder's hit, also on *Tighten Up Volume 1*.

● *Kansas City / Out The Light*
Joya Landis
Trojan TR 620 (1968)
produced by Duke Reid
A real party favourite also on *Tighten Up Volume 1* and *Here Comes The Duke* (TRL 6).

● *Win Your Love / All In The Game*
George A Penny / Val Bennett
Trojan TR 625 (November 1968)
produced by Lynford Anderson
Whatever happened to this guy??? One great record and then nothing else. This was yet another cover of an old Sam Cooke song and was featured on *Tighten Up Volume 1*.

● *No More Heartaches / I'll Follow You*
The Beltones
Trojan TR 628 (December 1968)
produced by Harry J
Reputedly Harry J's first production, this was one of reggae's earliest successes. Also the title track of Trojan's first compilation album of Harry J material (TTL 14).

- **Love Up, Kiss Up / Labba Labba Reggae (Lonely Goat Herd)**
The Termites / The Supersonics (but credited to Alton Ellis)
Trojan TR 634 (December 1968)
produced by Duke Reid
An early slice of suggestive reggae also on *Here Comes The Duke*.

- **Moonlight Lover / I Love You True**
Joya Landis
Trojan TR 641 (January 1969)
produced by Duke Reid
The third and last solo record from Joya, unless she continued her recording career under a different name. Organist Winston Wright cut it as *Moonlight Groover* on Trojan (TR 7701) and four years later Dennis Alcapone DJ'd it as
Wake Up Jamaica for yet another of his
number one hits in the reggae listings.
Moonlight Lover was justifiably put on *Tighten
Up Volume 2* and Trojan's *Moonlight Groover*
compilation of Duke Reid cuts (TTL 31).

- **Love Is All I Had / Boys And Girls**
Reggae
Phyllis Dillon
Trojan TR 651 (March 1969)
produced by Duke Reid
A very highly-rated record now, largely thanks
to frequent spins at London's sadly defunct
Treasure Isle Club a few years back. Never
included on album.

- *Fattie Fattie / Last Call (aka Tribute To Drumbago)*
Clancy Eccles / The Silverstars
Trojan TR 658 (May 1969)
produced by Clancy Eccles
A very repetitive record, but who said repetition was boring? Classic rude reggae which compels the listener to keep on listening, Trojan made sure they milked it for all it was worth - it was on *Tighten Up Volume 2* (natch), and Clandisc's *Herbsman Reggae* and *Freedom* LPs. The flip also came out on Nu-Beat (NB 030) as *Tribute To Drumbago* (credited in this case to The Dynamites) but was slightly different.

Above: The Upsetters and The Pioneers arrive in the UK for their 1970 tour billed as "The Greatest Reggae Package Tour In The World."

- *Woman Capture Man / One (One Heart, One Love)*
The Ethiopians
Trojan TR 666 (June 1969)
produced by JJ Johnson
A big one in the discos. Featured on both The Ethiopians' Trojan LPs, *Reggae Power* and *Woman Capture Man*.

- *Long Shot Kick The Bucket / Jumping The Gun*
The Pioneers / Reco
Trojan TR 672 (1969)
produced by Leslie Kong
A UK Top Thirty hit which brought the group to this country for an "All Star Reggae Package Tour" along with most of the other JA outfits who saw chart action in '69. This was raw, undiluted reggae which broke out of the clubs and into the best sellers. There's very little comparison with this and their Top Five, *Let Your Yeah Be Yeah* a couple of years later, by which time The Pioneers had gone totally commercial. *Long Shot Kick The Bucket* was featured on the classic Pioneers' LP of the same name (TBL 103), *Reggae Chartbusters Volume 1*, and *Tighten Up Volume 2*. And yes, copies of the single were briefly pressed with the old all-orange Trojan label, possibly because the company had run out of custom orange and white labels. They do exist, believe me!

- *Ease Up / You're Gonna Feel It*
The Bleechers
Trojan TR 679 (1969)
produced by Lee Perry
One of the few really popular Trojan singles not to appear on a compilation. The Bleechers were a superb group and I've yet to hear a duff side from them.

- *Sweet Sensation / It's My Delight*
The Melodians
Trojan TR 695 (1969)
produced by Leslie Kong
Actually issued as a double A side, this was a small chart hit in the UK (no. 41). The Melodians were the only major reggae act on Trojan's books who never had an LP released by the company, which is all the more strange given that *Sweet Sensation* was such a strong seller. It was however on three compilations - *Reggae Chartbusters Volume 1*, *Reggae, Reggae, Reggae*, and the Leslie Kong compilation, *Hot Shots Of Reggae* (TBL 128). Ansel Collins did a straightforward organ version of it entitled *Cotton Dandy* (TR 7712) which was mildly successful for him. A long awaited Melodians compilation was eventually brought out in 1980.

- *Pressure Drop / Smoke Screen*
The Maytals / Beverley's All Stars
Trojan TR 7709 (1969)
produced by Leslie Kong
The first in a series of very successful sides for them on Trojan's main label. *Pressure Drop* was pretty much in the gospel-tinged rousing style for which they became so famous. It was also released on Pyramid (PYR 6073) and volume one of *The Trojan Story*. This is the first disc reviewed in Trojan's new "7700" series, which was created largely because of the similarity of the numerical sequence of the former "600" series with those used by some of the company's other subsidiaries.

Monkey Man / Night And Day
The Maytals
Trojan TR 7711 (1969)
produced by Leslie Kong
Very different from *Pressure Drop*, *Monkey Man* was a much more jaunty, singalong affair. It nudged into the bottom 40 of the UK Charts in May 1970, but had been out for a good few months before that. The chart placing tied in well with their appearance at Wembley's International Reggae Festival that month. *Monkey Man* was also included on their Trojan LP of the same name (TBL 107), *Tighten Up Volume 3*, *Reggae, Reggae, Reggae* and *Hot Shots Of Reggae*. Ken Lazarus covered the song rather badly for JA's Federal Records and it saw release in the UK on London's Reggae series.

- *Virgin Soldier / Brixton Reggae Festival*
Hot Rod All Stars / The Setters (but actually The Hot Rod All Stars)
Trojan TR 7733 (1970)
produced by Lambert Briscoe (UK)
Another sparkling organ effort from South of the River and preferable to their other 45 on Trojan's main label, *Strong Man* (TR 7732).

- *Barbwire / Calypso Mama*
Nora Dean / The Barons
Trojan TR 7735 (1970)
produced by Byron Smith
I couldn't believe my ears when I first heard this. A song about a boy with barbwire in his underpants sung to The Techniques' *You Don't Care* rhythm. This was by far Nora's biggest hit, although her recorded output was comparatively small. Beware her *Must Get A Man* on High Note which sounds juicy, but was actually calypso. *Barbwire* was on *Tighten Up Volume 3* and *Lochness Monster*.

- *Water Melon / She's My Scorcher*
The Maytals
Trojan TR 7757 (1970)
produced by Leslie Kong
The public actually went more for the flip, although both are good solid tracks. *She's My Scorcher* was on *Hot Shots Of Reggae* and their *Monkey Man* album. *Water Melon* was only made available again via an Attack label compilation in 1988.

- *54-46 Was My Number / Version*
The Maytals / Beverley's All Stars
Trojan TR 7808 (December 1970)
produced by Leslie Kong
A song they originally cut in 1968 which saw release on Pyramid (PYR 6030) and later Trojan (TR 7726) as the flip to *Sweet And Dandy* (also issued on Pyramid!). *54-46 Was My Number* made the transition from rock steady to reggae very well and, perhaps because this was the first version I heard, it has always been my preferred cut. The large gap between this selected item's catalogue number and the last one's, reveals that very little skinhead reggae was by then being put out on the main Trojan label, it having been largely given over to commercial pop reggae.
Included on the highly successful first volume of *Club Reggae*.

Tropical

This was initially a subsidiary of Bamboo during '71-'72 but was later re-launched by Creole Records in the mid-Seventies with an orange and black swirly label. The only release worth picking up out of Bamboo's batch of 15 releases is Dennis Alcapone's *False Profit* (with Max Romeo's *Rude Medley* on the flip). Most sides were produced by Ken Chang of Tropical's Jamaican counterpart, but certainly aren't up to the standards of the island's other great production men of the time (sorry Ken). Like Ackee, each issue came with a different colour label depicting a palm tree, from mauve and turquoise to green, bronze and red. Definitely Bamboo's least attractive subsidiary.

Unity

The final Pama subsidiary in this chapter, Unity was a real Bunny Lee powerhouse with around 40 of its 71 releases being his productions. It was also the UK counterpart of Lee's Jamaican Unity label and both label designs were very similar. Kicking off with Stranger Cole And Tommy McCook's *Last Flight To Reggae City* (UN 501), the label immediately became one of the main British outlets specialising in the up-and-coming sound of reggae. Among the UK's top reggae sounds of December '68 and January '69 were *Last Flight To Reggae City*, Lester Sterling And Stranger Cole's *Bangarang* (UN 502), and Slim Smith's multi-versioned *Everybody Needs Love* (UN 504).

These first few tracks were versioned time and time again by Lee for subsequent Unity outings and it's fair to say that the label is a real feast for the version buff. The UK release of Max Romeo's infamous *Wet Dream* was delayed for a few months due to problems surrounding its title and lyrical content (no surprise here!), although it did of course go on to become a UK Top Tenner in Mid-'69. Romeo's follow-up, *Mini Skirt Vision*, was nowhere near as good and, although a strong seller on the back of *Wet Dream*, was bland dirty postcard stuff.

Bunny Lee productions on Unity were always put together well for Pama LPs. Slim Smith's *Everybody Needs Love* package contains most of his Unity sides and is still available on repress today. Now unavailable, Lester Sterling's *Bangarang* compilation of his Unity tracks is superb and features the very sexy Eunice Cooke - aka Miss Unity Records on the front cover. A compilation of Unity 45s (*Unity's Greatest Hits*) was also issued.

Although most of Unity's output is of Jamaican origin, one gem to cast a special eye out for is Laurel Aitken's *Donkey Man* from early '69, which is neatly tucked away on the flipside of Tommy McCook's *The Avengers* (itself an instrumental version of *Bangarang*). The song, with its references to jumping on the donkey train and the lady from Stamford Hill, is presumably about Dandy and his relationship with Rita King, who he effectively ditched after Trojan took him under its wing. It's an excellent track - almost a spoken story in thick Jamaican patois - which shows the way some of his later sides on Nu-Beat were to go.

Unity started to lose impetus during 1970 when some of the Bunny Lee material began to get a bit weak (it was almost as though he was giving his best stuff to Trojan's Jackpot subsidiary). It soldiered on with a mish-mash of UK and JA stuff and, as with some of the other Pama subsidiaries, lost its way along with its reputation as an outlet for skinhead reggae par excellence.

A lot of its later output, like Lester Sterling's *Slip Up*, were versions of Lee's '69 rhythms (in this case Slim Smith's *Slip Away*), and were old hat by the time they surfaced. One of the best discs from the final stages of Unity was a reissue of two

Derrick Morgan cuts from '68 (*The Conqueror / Bedweight* on UN 569) which, given the age of the tracks, must have sold next to nothing at the time. Which is a real pity as the B side is unavailable almost anywhere else.

- **Bangarang / If We Should Ever Meet**
Lester Sterling And Stranger Cole / Stranger Cole
Unity UN 502 (December 1968)
produced by Bunny Lee
Another of reggae's early successes and one which further consolidated Pama as the label with the "Boss Sounds" reputation. This was at the top of the reggae charts during Christmas '68. Basically just a fast, infectious jerky horns instrumental, with Stranger singing "Muma no wan' Bangarang" over the top. Also on Lester's *Bangarang* LP (SECO 15), *Unity's Greatest Hits* (ECO 7) and *Reggae Hits '69 Volume 1* (ECO 3).

- **Wet Dream / She's But A Little Girl**
Max Romeo
Unity UN 503 (1969)
produced by Bunny Lee
According to Pama, *Wet Dream* was issued somewhat later than the other initial Unity releases due to its controversial title and subject matter. But even a blanket radio ban couldn't keep this one from reaching the UK Top Fifty in a lengthy chart run lasting from May to November. It reputedly sold 250,00 copies in the process. Utilising Derrick Morgan's *Hold You Jack* rhythm (see Island listing), it heralded Maxie's nationwide tour later that year. Unfortunately, the success of *Wet Dream* meant that he soon became tarred with an uncomfortable rude reggae brush. There were some further cash-in discs on Unity of a similar nature (eg *Wine Her Goosie* and *Mini Skirt Vision*), but it took him some years to shake off the rude image. Ironically, when his career took off again in the early Seventies, many of his generally "rootsy" tunes came to prominence because of their brilliant social commentary and witty lyrics. *Wet Dream* was included on his Pama LP, *A Dream* (PMLP 15), which certainly had its high and low points, *Bang Bang Lulu* and *This Is Reggae Volume 1*.

- **Everybody Needs Love / Come Back Girl**
Slim Smith / Junior Smith
Unity UN 504 (January 1969)
produced by Bunny Lee / Junior Smith (UK)
Another big selling single that made Slim and the Unity label such a big draw with the skinhead fraternity. Bunny Lee versioned the rhythm dozens of times, and many of these were put on Trojan's *Now That's What I And I Call Version* compilation in December 1989. It was originally included on four Pama albums - Slim's classic LP set of the same name (ECO 9), *Unity's Greatest Hits* (ECO 7), *A Gift From Pama* (SECO 20), and *Sixteen Dynamic Reggae Hits* (PMP 2015).

- **The Avengers / Donkey Man**
Tommy McCook / Laurel Aitken
Unity UN 506 (1969)
produced by Bunny Lee / Laurel Aitken (UK)
The flipside of this has already been mentioned above. *The Avengers* was included on Pama's *The Lovely Dozen* (PSP 1001).

Opposite page: Max Romeo at Reggae Sunsplash, 1992 (photo by Maverick)

- *Slip Away / Spanish Harlem*
Slim Smith
Unity UN 520 (1969)
produced by Bunny Lee
Another soulful reggae cover of a Ben E King number, Bunny Lee also gave this rhythm to Lee Perry for him to use on Dave Barker's *Prisoner Of Love* (see Punch label listing). *Slip Away* was included on Slim's *Everybody Needs Love* album.

- *Derrick Top-The-Pop / Capone's Revenge*
Derrick Morgan / Glen Adams
Unity UN 540 (1969)
produced by Derrick Morgan
Heavily influenced by Andy Capp's *Pop A Top* on Treasure Isle. Also on the Pama albums *This Is Reggae Volume 1* and Derrick's *Moon Hop*.

- *Clap Clap / You've Got Your Troubles*
Max Romeo & The Hippy Boys / Max Romeo
Unity UN 545 (1970)
produced by Bunny Lee
Largely a reggae version of The Wailers' *Put It On* on Island (WI 268). Unity started losing its way around the time this was released.

- *Return Of Jack Slade / Fat Man*
Derrick Morgan
Unity UN 546 (1970)
produced by Derrick Morgan (UK)
A skinhead reggae favourite containing references to London, Birmingham and Liverpool but also taking influences from King Stitt's *The Ugly One*. Included on Pama's mega-rare *Young, Gifted And Black* compilation LP (ECO 35).

- *Walking Along / Warfare*
John Holt / Donald Lee (with Jackie Mittoo and Bunny Lee's All Stars)
Unity UN 552 (1970)
produced by Bunny Lee
The B side, *Warfare*, easily out-shone John Holt's pedestrian effort. Donald Lee was a DJ very much in the style of Count Machuki , leading some commentators to suggest that either the credits were wrong or he was one and the same. *Warfare* uses the same rhythm employed on Bunny Lee All Stars' *Hook Up* (UN 533) which featured Jackie Mittoo.

- *More Balls / Bum Ball*
Mark Anthony And The Jets / Tony King
Unity UN 565 (1970)
produced by Derrick Morgan (UK)
Don't be misled by the unfortunate title as this is pretty good stuff. It's a DJ version of Lloyd And Devon's equally bizzarely-titled *Red Bum Ball*, which came out on Island (WI 3094) and was later used by I Roy for *Hot Bomb* issued on Green Door (GD 4030) and included on *Tighten Up Volume 6* (TBL 185). The rhythm was laid in JA so its really a half-JA, half-UK production.

Up-front

This label appears - though it isn't actually 100% confirmed - to have been put out by Beacon, which was a bit of a jack of all trades effort concentrating mainly on blues and soul from Black Velvet, Sons And Lovers, Ram John Holder (he of *Desmond's* fame), and The Showstoppers, although it also did a neat line in budget type LPs. On the other hand, some of the Upfront titles were credited to Revolution Music, so it might conceivably have been put out by that label.

Upfront put out albums by Sugar Simone (aka Tito Simon) and Joyce Bond And The Colour Supplement, neither of which were up to much. In fact, the only good thing about the Simone LP is the sleeve notes, which give a good historical account of the man's career. There were a few singles, such as Owen Gray And The Maximum Breed's *Mudda Granma Reggae / Dream Lover* (UPF3) and Simone's *Turn On The Heatwave / Crying Blues* (UP 1) from '69.

Upsetter

This is the final label covered in this and appropriately enough is the last of the Trojan / B & C subsidiaries. As Trojan's exclusive outlet for JA productions from Lee Perry, aka Scratch The Upsetter, it is a fairly straightforward label to deal with. It is best known for the Upsetters' *Return of Django*, which rose to number five in the UK best sellers during the latter months of '69.

Above: The Upsetters

The Upsetters were Lee Perry's studio session band and, as such, were responsible for a large chunk of the Upsetter label's output. There were some cracking organ instrumentals issued by the band, like *Cold Sweat, Live Injection* and *The Vampire*, which also contained some storming vocals on the flip sides from The Bleechers (*Pound Get A Blow, Everything For Fun* and *Check Him Out* respectively).

There were several LPs issued on Upsetter, namely *Return of Django* (TRL 19), which contains the title track and some of the best Upsetters tracks from the label's early stages, *Scratch The Upsetter Again* (TTL 28), which showed a slower,

145

moodier edge to The Upsetters music, and *Eastwood Rides Again* (TBL 125), which was a patchy affair containing several purely bass and drum tracks lacking in any real substance. There were also a few uncredited vocal tracks on *Eastwood Rides Again*, which is one of the rarest Trojan albums ever issued.

There was another all-Upsetters LP (*The Good, The Bad And The Upsetters*) put out on the main Trojan label, but it was produced over in the UK by Bruce Anthony rather than Lee Perry and was a pretty naff affair overall. Other LPs issued on Upsetter were by Bob Marley And The Wailers and Dave Barker (with The Upsetters).

Singles-wise, Upsetter label releases are extremely rare and, with as many as five singles by The Upsetters appearing consecutively, it's not surprising that so many of them slipped through the net. The biggest sellers (aside from *Return Of Django*) were The Upsetters' follow-up *Live Injection*, The Bleechers' *Come Into My Parlour* (both of these were on *Tighten Up Volume Two*), Dave Barker And The Upsetters' *Shocks Of Mighty* (also put out on Pama's Punch label), and Bob Marley And The Wailers' *Duppy Conqueror* and *Small Axe*.

The label was discontinued by Trojan in '73 and the company's Perry output was put out on Attack and (for a short time) Down Town. Towards the end of its life, Upsetter issues veered more towards rootsier "back to Africa" stuff like Junior Byles' *Beat Down Babylon* and *Place Called Africa*, and Dennis Alcapone And Niney's *Babylon's Burning*. There was little here to interest any skinhead. Perry's other issuing labels around the mid-Seventies were Ethnic, Cactus and DIP, where his music was very much in the psychedelic dub vein.

- **Return Of Django / Dollar In The Teeth**
The Upsetters
Upsetter US 301 (1969)
produced by Lee Perry
The infectious rhythm of *Return Of Django* caught Joe Public's attention in the autumn of '69 and it was sent rocketing all the way to the number five spot in the UK charts. Val Bennett played lead sax on it but he, in common with all Upsetters releases, was just an uncredited session musician. It was included on the LP of the same name on Upsetter (TRL 15), Trojan's *Tighten Up Volume 2*, and *Reggae Chartbusters Volume 1*. Trojan made a curious decision four years later when they released Neville Grant's superb vocal version of *Return Of Django* on Down Town (entitled *Sick And Tired*).

- *What A Price / How Can I Forget?*
Busty Brown
Upsetter US 304 (1969)
produced by Lee Perry
A forgotten / unheard classic, this is a version of a Fats Domino song. My copy got irreparably damaged ten years ago and I've been looking for a replacement ever since.

- *Badam Bam / Medical Operation*
The Ravers / The Upsetters
Upsetter US 312 (1969)
produced by Lee Perry
The vocal cut to *Live Injection*. Great, great, great!

- **Live Injection / Everything For (Your) Fun**

The Upsetters / The Bleechers

Upsetter US 313 (December 1969)

produced by Lee Perry

Although enjoying good sales, this unfortunately failed to repeat the success of *Return Of Django* (although to be fair it was radically different). Live Injection features some brilliant organ work courtesy of Glen Adams and builds into a stunning crescendo. Also on the LPs *Tighten Up Volume 2* and *Return Of Django*.

- **Come Into My Parlour / Dry Your Tears**

The Bleechers / The Mellotones

Upsetter US 314 (1969)

produced by Lee Perry

A great choice for inclusion on *Tighten Up Volume 2*. Glen Adams is in their again tinkling the ivories.

- **Cold Sweat / Pound Get A Blow**

The Upsetters / The Bleechers

Upsetter US 316 (1969)

produced by Lee Perry

"Take off your jacket and sock it to me" goes Lee Perry's spoken introduction. Another Glen Adams special also known as *Power Cut* (see Gas listing). The flip was good too and is about the conversion of the British-oriented Jamaican Pound into the Dollar currency. All good topical stuff. Roland Alphonso later cut it as *Roll On* for release on Punch (PH 39).

- **The Vampire / Check Him Out**

The Upsetters / The Bleechers

Upsetter US 317 (1969)

produced by Lee Perry

The flip was probably the more popular of the two and extolled the musical virtues of King Scratch himself. It's a pity The Bleechers have never been committed to an album of their own.

- **Shocks Of Mighty / Set Me Free**

Dave Barker And The Upsetters

Upsetter US 331 (1970)

produced by Lee Perry

Another rhythm Perry gave to Bunny Lee. Also issued as a 45 on Punch (PH 25) and later included on Pama's *Sixteen Dynamic Reggae Hits*. On Trojan's *Tighten Up Volume 3* and Dave and the Upsetters' *Prisoner Of Love* LP on Upsetter (TBL 127).

A
"DREAM"
COME TRUE
FOR
MAX ROMEO
NOW TOP TWENTY
IN THE B.B.C. CHARTS
HEAR IT - BUY IT
PAMA/UNITY-503
Pleasant Dreams

INDEX

For ease of reference, we have included an index of artists, producers and labels that can be found in this book. Individual artists and producers are generally listed by surname, except in the case of obvious stage names (eg Prince Buster can be found under P).

F

Fab, 6, 32, 43, 56, 57, 65, 81, 82, 94, 109, 114, 135
Fabions, The, 59
Faith, 21
Family Circle, 51
Fay & Matador, 26
Federal Records, 139
Federals, The, 60, 94
Fight, 38
Fitzroy (Sterling) And Harry (Young), 132
Flames, The, 71, 99, 104, 129, 130
Foster, Calva L, 35, 37
Foster, Keith, 35
Foster, Les, 35, 37, 55, 128
Foster, Vincent, 79
Four Gees, The, 118
Four Lads And A Lass, 51
Francis, Winston, 110, 116
Freddie Notes And The Rudies, 87, 114, 134
Freedom Singers, The, 13, 18, 71, 103

G

G G, 60, 81, 85, 126
G G All Stars, The, 32, 80, 81
G G (George) Grossett, 69
G G Rhythm Section, 58
Gardner, Boris, 76, 129
Gas, 5, 16, 17, 18, 43, 81, 82, 84, 85, 96, 104, 118, 120, 147
Gayfeet, 15, 43, 71, 87, 89
Gaylads, The, 29, 54, 65, 70, 89, 90, 93, 98, 116, 133
Gaylettes, The, 101
Gaytones, The, 89, 90
George Lee & The Rudies, 75
George Lee And The Music Doctors, 97
Giant, 43, 86, 119,
Gibbs, Joe, 13, 29, 48, 49, 51, 57, 71, 72, 85, 108, 109
Gibson, Joel, 48
Girlie, 26, 48, 100, 105, 106, 129
Girlie And Paul, 48
Glade Soul, 121
Gladiators, The, 72, 116, 117, 123
Glen (Adams) And Dave (Barker), 88
Goodall, Graeme, 15, 37, 45, 51, 99, 115, 129, 132
Gophtal, Lee, 11, 13, 17, 18, 35
Grant, Eddy, 34, 46

Grape, 15, 38, 43, 87, 88
Gray, Owen, 9, 20, 29, 33, 35, 41, 46, 48, 60, 64, 108, 110, 114, 116, 126, 145
Green Door, 43, 88, 144
Gregory, Tony, 65, 70
Greyhound, 39, 134
Griffiths, Marcia, 65, 67, 93
Groov(e)y, Winston, 34, 51, 67, 87, 96, 103
Gruvy Beats, The, 105

H

Hadfield, Dave, (D & H Productions), 116
Hamboys, The, 65
Hammers, The, 118
Hannibal, Lance, 35, 57
Harmonians, The, 101
Harriott, Derrick, 11, 15, 16, 20, 30, 55, 60, 69, 80, 93, 94, 119, 120, 121, 134
Harris, Wynonie, 9
Harry And Radcliffe, 62
Harry J, 18, 27, 30, 43, 88,
Harry J All Stars, The, 16, 30, 88
Hawk, Graham, 107
Hazel And The Jolly Boys, 71
Henry And Liza, 26
Henry III, 94
Heptones, The, 21, 25, 29, 52, 59, 65, 109, 122, 123
Herman, Bongo, 120
Hibbert, Toots, 124
Higgs, Joe, 118
Higgs And Wilson, 11, 63
High Note, 5, 13, 15, 31, 43, 71, 89, 90, 98, 130, 140
Hillcrest, 43, 90, 101
Hinds, Justin, 11, 25, 130, 132
Hinds, Neville, 121
Hinds, Winston, 5
Hippy Boys, The, 31, 49, 58, 62, 89, 90, 144
Hala-Gala, 7, 43, 45, 117
Holder, Ram John, 145
Holder, Frank, 10
Holt, John, 17, 21, 31, 78, 93, 96, 109, 123, 124, 129, 130, 144
Honeyboy Martin And The Voices, 59
Hornet, 43
Horse, 17, 37, 43, 90, 113
Hot Lead, 43, 90
Hot Rod, 16, 34, 43, 87, 92,
Hot Rod All Stars, The, 34, 75, 92, 128, 140
Hot Shot, 43, 57, 92, 139, 140
Hudson, Keith, 119, 122
Hugh, Sang, 21

Hughes, Alex - see Judge Dread

I

I Roy, 24, 31, 58, 59, 88, 102, 111, 134, 144
Impersonators, The, 97
Inner Mind, 90, 118
Inspirations, The, 31, 60, 136
Isaacs, David, 136
Isaacs, Gregory, 111
Island, 7, 10, 11, 12, 13, 15, 16, 25, 29, 30, 31, 33, 35, 37, 41, 42, 43, 44, 45, 46, 48, 52, 65, 67, 68, 74, 76, 92, 93, 94, 95, 113, 118, 122, 129, 133, 136, 143, 144

J

J. N. A. C., 43
J-Dan, 16, 37, 43, 80, 97, 98
J J, 43, 71, 76, 98, 99, 111
J J All Stars, The, 99, 117
Jack And The Beanstalks, 126, 127
Jackie Mittoo And The Soul Brothers, 93
Jackie Mittoo And The Soul Vendors, 122
Jackpot, 15, 27, 31, 34, 38, 43, 62, 96, 97, 141
Jackson, Siggy, 64, 114
Jaguar, 42, 43
Jah Stitch, 24
Jah Woosh, 24
Jamaican Actions, The, 123
James, Bobby, 97
James, Winston, 92
Jay Boy, 43, 88, 118
Jay Boys, The, 88
Jet Star, 20
Jimmy London & The Inspirations, 136
Jiving Juniors, The, 11, 30
Joe Gibbs' All Stars, The, 51
Jo Jo Bennett And The Fugitives, 72
Joe, 38, 43, 87, 92, 99, 100, 118, 128
Joe's (Mansano's) Record Shack, 6, 38
Joe's All Stars, 38, 99, 100
Joe The Boss, 100
Johnson, "Sir" J J, 32, 71, 72, 98, 99, 111, 116, 117, 138
Johnson, Carey, 67
Johnson, Harry "J", 18, 27, 30, 75, 76, 79, 88, 118, 133, 136
Jolly, 43, 45, 100, 119
Jonas, Melanie, 122
Jordan, Louis, 9
Joyce Bond And The Colour Supplement, 145
Judge Dread, 24, 25, 26, 27, 54, 56, 100, 113

Jump-Up, 25, 44
Junior, 44, 90, 101
Justin Hinds & The Dominoes, 11, 130, 132

K

Kalypso, 10, 44
Kassner, Ed, 42, 43, 44, 45, 118
Keith And Enid, 11, 67, 93
Keith And Tex, 30, 94, 121
Kelly, Pat, 5, 17, 18, 31, 76, 82, 84, 85, 86, 96, 120, 127, 129
Kent Walker And The All Stars, 117
Khouri, Ken, 33
King, 44
King, Benny, 86
King, Benny and Rita, 33, 35
King, Tony, 101, 144
King, Peter, 68
King, Rita, 141
King Cannon, 75, 76, 79, 90, 101, 107
King Horror, 26, 34, 87, 99, 115
King Reggie, 115
King Sporty, 54
King Stitt, 24, 29, 54, 62, 63, 76, 144
King Tapper, 38
Kingstonians, The, 22, 30, 54, 55, 69, 72, 117, 120, 121, 126, 127, 134
Kong, Leslie, 30, 31, 33, 64, 93, 99, 111, 113, 124, 126, 133, 138, 139, 140

L

Laing, Denzil, 67
Landis, Joya, 56, 130, 133, 136, 137
Larry and Alvin, 67, 123
Lawrence, Larry, 21, 23, 37, 43, 96, 128
Lazarus, Ken, 101, 139
Leaders, The, 48
Lee, Bunny, 15, 16, 17, 18, 21, 24, 31, 35, 39, 57, 59, 62, 64, 79, 84, 85, 86, 93, 94, 95, 96, 97, 110, 119, 120, 133, 136, 141, 143, 144, 147
Lee, Byron, 76, 77, 78, 79, 107, 117, 133, 134
Lee, Don Tony, 64
Lee, Donald, 144
Lee, George, 75, 97
Levy, Carl, 18, 92
Lewis, Alva, 57
Lewis, Hopeton, 62, 77, 93
Limbo, 44,
Lincoln, Junior, 20, 21, 41, 42, 44, 48, 101
Lindo, Earl "Wire", 78

O

Ocean, 44
Opel, Jackie, 25
Opening, The, 115
Ove, Horace, 132
Owen Gray and Sir Collins And His Band, 64

P

Pablo, Augustus, 70
Page One, 42
Palmer Brothers (Harry, Carl, Jeff), 17, 20, 60, 104, 117
Pama, 3, 12, 16, 17, 18, 20, 21, 22, 23, 25, 26, 27, 29, 31, 33, 34, 35, 42, 43, 44, 45, 46, 47, 55, 58, 60, 62, 67, 68, 69, 70, 79, 80, 81, 82, 84, 85, 90, 94, 96, 102, 103, 104, 105, 106, 107, 108, 109, 110, 117, 118, 123, 126, 141, 143, 144, 146, 147
Pama Dice, 34, 51, 100, 115
Pama Dice And Cummie, 80
Pama Supreme, 44, 108, 126
Paradise, 21
Paragons, The, 32, 78, 93, 129, 130
Parker, Ken, 20, 48, 52, 86, 122
Pat Kelly And The Uniques, 86, 120
Patrick and Lloyd, 55, 56
Patsy, 5, 11, 31, 70, 89, 92
Patsy And Delano Stewart, 89
Patsy And Peggy, 92
Paul, Eugene, 108
Paula And The Jetliners, 114
Paulette & Gee, 60, 85
Pavement, The, 70
Peaches, The, 16
Penguin, 21
Penny, George A, 136
Pereira, Ray, 51
Perry, Lee, 15, 16, 29, 31, 48, 49, 54, 60, 72, 85, 93, 107, 109, 110, 111, 116, 122, 126, 133, 136, 139, 144, 145, 146, 147
Peter Tosh & The Wailers, 93
Phase Four, 81
Philligree, 51, 129, 132
Pioneers, The, 15, 16, 29, 35, 48, 49, 51, 59, 75, 108, 111, 124, 133, 134, 138
Planetone, 44, 45
Port-o-Jam, 44
Pottinger, Sonia, 13, 15, 31, 70, 71, 87, 89, 90, 98
Pratt, Phil, 32, 96, 101

President, 38, 41, 42, 43, 44, 45, 70, 85, 104, 118
Pressure Beat, 30, 44, 51, 108, 109
Prete, Chris, 32
Prince Buster, 6, 11, 12, 26, 31, 32, 56, 57, 65, 71, 81, 82, 104, 109, 114, 117, 118
Prince Buster & The All Stars, 57, 81, 82
Prince Buster (label), 26, 44, 109
Prince Jazzbo, 24, 127
Prince Of Darkness, 75, 99
Proby, P J, 81
Prophets, The, 55, 56
Pullen, Mark - see Pyramid Press
Punch, 17, 20, 29, 31, 44, 56, 62, 85, 109, 110, 111, 130, 144, 146, 147
Pyramid, 12, 15, 16, 18, 43, 44, 71, 111, 113, 139, 140
Pyramid Press, 2
Pyramids, The, 41, 64, 70, 71, 104, 118

Q

Q, 16, 44, 114

R

R & B, 11, 33, 35, 42, 43, 44, 45, 59, 70, 90, 100, 101, 102, 118, 119, 121
Race Fans, The, 133
Rainbow, 44, 104, 114, 118
Randy's, 45, 59, 115
Ranglin, Alvin, 32, 57, 58, 60, 62, 80, 81, 85, 109
Record Corner, 6
Regent, George, 58
Reggae (label) 38, 45, 115, 139
Reggae Boys, The, 29, 85, 110
Reggaeites, The, 70
Reid, Nehemia, 39
Revolution, 44, 45, 116, 145
Revolution Music, 145
Rhino, 45, 116
Rhoden, Pat, 102, 108
Rhythm Rulers, The, 58
Richards, Cynthia, 63, 107, 109
Richards, Roy, 54
Riding, Jackie, 81
Riley, Desmond, 37, 75
Riley, Winston, 32, 60, 72, 75, 127
Riley, Martin, 57, 82, 84
Riley's All Stars, 60
Rio, 12, 15, 45, 116, 117
Roberts, Sonny, 44, 45

S

Also Now Available

In 1979, The Specials burst onto the British music scene and changed it forever. For two glorious years, The Specials and friends down at 2 Tone HQ ruled the nation's airwaves and dance floors. And then, shortly after *Ghost Town* had given them their biggest hit to date, the band suddenly split.

This is the story of those glorious years and what has happened to the band members since. *You're Wondering Now - A History Of The Specials* is not only the first book of its kind to document the band's history, but it also pays equal attention to the bands that followed in its wake - Fun Boy Three, The Special A.K.A., JB's Allstars, The Colour Field, Vegas, and so the list goes on. Complete with full Specials discography, it's a must for anyone whose soul has been ska'd for life by Coventry's finest.

You're Wondering Now
A History Of The Specials
By Paul Williams (Editor of *Street Feeling* Fanzine)

You're Wondering Now - A History Of The Specials can be ordered from the best specialist music and clothing shops and any good bookshop (and even most of the bad ones too). It can also be ordered direct from the publisher. For ordering details and a copy of our latest catalogue, please write to the address below.

S.T. Publishing
P.O. Box 12, Dunoon, Argyll. PA23 7BQ. Scotland.

If you enjoyed this book, there's a good chance that you'll like our other titles . . .

Since 1991, S.T. Publishing has specialised in documenting street music and street youth cults. Out of the thousands of books published every year, very few are aimed at street culture, and fewer still written from within the scene rather than by outsiders. So we took it upon ourselves to put the boot back into literature so to speak. If you would like a copy of our latest catalogue, just write to the address below and ask for one. We send books to customers all over the world and do our very best to fill orders as soon as they arrive.

Meanwhile, coming soon . . .

ONE FOR THE ROAD
By Kid Stoker

Kid Stoker, of Red London fame, has put his pint glass down long enough to pen this debut novel which follows the fortunes of punk band, The Outlaws, as they set out for one more tour of Europe before calling it a day. Hilarious stuff it is too - and probably the funniest book you'll read all year.

NIGHTSHIFT
By Pete McKenna

Pete McKenna and his friends were regulars at the Wigan Casino, a mecca for fans of northern soul music. This is his personal account of the northern scene as it was in the glory days when all that mattered was dancing all night to the greatest sounds around.

For full release details on the above books and a copy of our latest 16 page catalogue packed with books by Richard Allen, Steve Goodman (check out the superb *England Belongs To Me* if punk rock's your cup of tea), George Marshall and others, please write to the address below.

S.T. Publishing
P.O. Box 12, Dunoon, Argyll. PA23 7BQ. Scotland.